TEN **MILES** TO YOUR
DESTINY

PRESSING TOWARDS THE MARK.

MALCOLM BROWN

Unless otherwise stated, all Scripture quotations come from the King James Version of the Bible.

Malcolm Brown
Tmtydthebook@gmail.com

© Copyright 2018 Malcolm Brown
ISBN: 978-1-943342-22-8

PublishAffordably.com
773.783.2981 | Chicago, Illinois

DEDICATION

I dedicate this book to my family, friends, and all those who support me. I thank you all for believing in me and always encouraging me to keep moving forward. I also want to thank my staff who worked hard and diligently to make this a success. I thank God for insight, revelation, and just the opportunity to be used to help His people. I will be forever grateful and for your love, I share this book with you.

Thank you all again, and God bless you.

-Malcolm Brown

CONTENTS

INTRODUCTION

The Bible tells us in Proverbs 3:5-6 to "trust in the Lord with all your heart and lean not to your own understanding, but acknowledge him in all your ways, and he shall direct your path." So, that's precisely what I did, but you could have never told me I would end up here. I grew up on the Southside of Chicago in an underprivileged community where drugs and gangs were a familiar sight. As a young boy, I could only straddle the fence for so long before life decisions had to be made. Day by day, I wrestled with doing the rights things like praying, going to church, and helping the elder cut their grass and clean their garages. I also had to deal with the temptation of indulging in other activities around the block like gang banging and selling weed. I could only play the role for so long before it was going to catch up with me. Like many of us, I was living on the fence.

I found myself in dangerous situations that nearly cost me my life and my future. Although I didn't realize it at the time, I was being a leader among my peers and demonstrating an entrepreneurial spirit at such a young age. It was around the age of seventeen when I realized my life was spiraling out of control. I was losing myself in the street life and a world that consisted of smoking and partying. Emotions like anger and depression began to set in; could it be I was looking for something or someone? Could it be that one of the last memories I have of my father is when I was six years young? It was Christmas, and I was over to my grandmother's house on my father's side, and he was supposed to come see me.

After waiting for a long time, he never showed up. Finally, he called and said, "Tell your mom to come and get you. I'm home with my wife." Apparently, he had another family, and I started realizing how unimportant I was to him. It may have been the need for my older brother, but he was in no position to help me. I've always admired and looked up to him for protection. However, he wasn't around due to a crime he had committed that left him with a seven-year sentence in the penitentiary. I was a boy lost in the world with no identity. I felt alone, and my actions reflected that.

It was during my junior year that I became a high school dropout. I literally went from being on the fence to being trapped on one side of it. It was also during this time that I had stopped praying and going to church. I had given up on God, but God didn't give up on me. It was my mother who later found a program for me called Lincoln's Challenge. This was a good alternative program for at-risk youth. It was there I began praying again and taking my life seriously, and God began to put the pieces back together. I graduated from that program with my GED in addition to setting a record as the cadet to receive the most rewards. Wow! What an accomplishment, but that was only the beginning.

After coming home, I started tapping into my inner artist and began tattooing. This new chapter in my life I believe was the start of it all. Five years later I found myself on a beach in Hawaii, again praying because I couldn't believe I was there. I thank God for the opportunity to travel and work; I remember thinking to myself, *Wow. How did I get here?* "The high school dropout," I remember saying and then laughing. I was enjoying the breeze as I sat and looked at the water. It was like a whisper in my mind when I suddenly heard, "Destiny." This is destiny! It is the never-ending journey in life that will connect you with people, places, and opportunities all for the purpose of God using you for His glory. I had come to this realization, and it was such a profound feeling of excitement that came over me. I asked God what was next, and almost immediately, He spoke to me about this book. He began revealing the title, chapters, and the purpose of it all.

God began showing me that for centuries mankind has been on this quest to find the true meaning of life. Hundreds of generations asking the same questions: *God what were we put here for? What is our purpose? What is my destiny?* Many have been successful in finding their own true calling by allowing their passions in life to serve their soul, that, that resulted in them finding their destiny. Unfortunately, many others have failed. It raised another question in my mind: *Why?*

I recall once hearing a renowned speaker ask the question, "Where is the richest place in the world?" A room full of people grew silent, and suddenly one man yelled out, "Africa." "No, it would have to be Wall Street," another man answered. The speaker then replied commending them both for their answers because they both were good. "The richest place in the world is not Africa nor is it Wall Street; it's not the diamond mines or the banks." He went on to say, "The richest place in the world is the graveyard; there in those graves lie dreams never accomplished, goals never set, and destiny that was never met." He continued, "The average person dies with their purpose and never meets their destiny."

I realized there are a number of reasons why people don't make it to their destinies. Some may fall victim to circumstance, or they merely fold under the pressure of fear. One thing is for sure, we are all on this road called life, trying to make it to meet destiny. We hit these pitfalls because of adversity.

I remember when I wanted to quit and just give up because of the pitfalls of depression, poverty, and insecurities. I came to the realization that I can't give up now. I had to be willing to face more adversities and pitfalls because destiny was not a pit stop—it is a journey. I could have given up a long time ago, but I didn't, and here I am having a conversation with you. As you will see, it's not easy, but if you first believe and second don't stop, you will make it. This book is designed to guide you down this road we call life and help you pass by those pitfalls of the enemy; so buckle up, and let's get ready to embark on this journey together. Starting route now, it's 10 miles to your destiny.

CHAPTER ONE

DESTINY:

What is Destiny? God's PURPOSE

"The two most important days in your life are the day you are born, and the day you find out why." -Mark Twain

What is it? The inevitable or necessary fate to which a particular person or thing is destined; one's lot. A predetermined course of events considered as something beyond human power or control. The hidden power believed to control what will happen in the future; fate.

I've provided you with the definition of the word destiny, but what does it mean as we live day by day? Destiny is not this elusive, esoteric phenomenon that one believes is only for the great among us—it's not magic; it's a reality for all of us, and we were born with it. When God created man, He had a plan and gave us purpose and destiny. He had set a path before us and promised to lead us to our destiny; we just have to trust Him. God tells us in Proverbs 3:5-6, "Trust in the Lord with all your heart and lean not to your own understanding but acknowledge him in all your ways and he shall direct your path." I know this sounds like a cliché because growing up we heard it a million times. However, when you change your perspective and really understand what the scripture is saying, you'll see that we have an internal guide with external results. We must trust in God and follow the course set ahead. God is our GPS.

Making it to your destiny is based on your walk, belief, and faithfulness to the route God has set. What is the route? The direction God will take you. Your actions on that route will determine your progress. You see, destiny or your destination is the sum calculation of all the actions we've taken or actions we've done in the past. God will use all the things you've been through to get you there. Those actions are like seeds that take root and sprout, ready to give off the fruit. That fruit is destiny.

⦿ ACTION
"You do today what they are waiting to do tomorrow."

All action, every second has an account with time. Good action and bad action, they become your past because time is moving and ultimately dictates your future or present. Always remember every action has a reaction. Based on your action, the results can be great, or they can be a course of catastrophic events, causing a downward spiral that's damaging to your destiny. This is why we must always keep the positive action going. Think of it like this: If what I did in the past is hurting me today and if I change what I do today, it won't hurt me tomorrow. It's literally just making a small change to your day by what you do, and you'll begin to see results. It's so important to be conscious of all your actions. Keeping positive actions will cause a positive destiny. Action gives off both positive and negative energy. The ratio of positive energy that you give off is the amount you'll get back. This rule of action works in all walks of life—work, school, and relationships. Utilizing this concept will ensure a more delightful ride on the road to your destiny.

I started using this a while ago, just speaking positively to keep motivated. I spoke this positive affirmation to myself: "Today I will think, and I will do!" I know that sounds crazy, but I literally believed that if I could think positive thoughts, I would do positive things. Let me tell you, it's easier said than done. I found the motivation to keep trying when I read Proverbs 23:7, "For as he *thinketh* in his heart, so is he." I realized your thoughts would control your actions and your actions will determine your moments with destiny. God can give you this elaborate vision for life and the future, but if you don't believe it, then it won't happen. You'll find that you keep walking past the blessing that is rightfully yours.

Begin telling yourself, *Today, I will think, and today, I will do. I will think about the promise, and I will do everything I can to get it.* I know to some this may seem useless—it may seem like a waste of time because of your current situation. You may not have the money or the resources. You may not have the background, or maybe you don't believe you are qualified. I believe if you can get that thing in your mind, whatever it is you want, and just do; take action and then you'll begin to see that thing come to pass in your life. Too many people focus on their current reality and become defeated, letting go of their dreams and forgetting about their destiny. Always remember, "Reality is wrong. Dreams are right." A changed life starts with a changed mind. You have to believe your thoughts and put that thing into action; you have to DO!

I've always wanted to travel the world, so I would get travelers' magazines and look at the different places, admiring the landscapes. One of my favorite places was Hawaii. I loved how the palm trees looked and the beautiful flowers. I painted this picture in my mind of this beautiful beachfront view; I could see the waves, the birds, the beautiful sunset. I could even smell the air. I held on to that image in my mind and just worked pushing forward. When times got rough, I would say,

"If I could just make it to Hawaii." Then I would get back to work pushing forward.

Some years had gone by, and one day my phone rang. I heard this soft voice asking me if I would be interested in doing some work for them. As we continued conversing about the potential work to be done, she asked if I would be willing to travel. I said yes and then asked where the location was, to which she responded, "Honolulu, Hawaii." I was so shocked that I almost dropped the phone. She said, "We will fly you out all expenses paid if you are willing to come." Although I kept my composure, there was excitement in my voice when I responded, "Yes!" It was because of the picture I had painted in my mind that it was now coming to fruition. Not long after that conversation, I was sitting on a beach in Hawaii, looking at the sunset. "Today I will think, and I will do." I want you to take a moment and think of something you want or a place you want to go, paint that image in your mind, and make it clear. Then proclaim out loud, as loud as you can, "Today I will think and I will do!" Now go get it!

⚲ FIND YOURSELF
"Accept responsibility for your life. Know that it is you who will get you where you want to go, no one else." - Les Brown

Now we understand destiny and how our actions ultimately dictate our future, but how do we find out what our own individual destiny is? The answer to that question lies in you. You see, your destiny is based on who God created you to be. The secret to figuring out your destiny is to find yourself. We live in what I believe to be a microwave world today. Our culture loves to promote overnight successes and desirable results. This culture pushes people to change themselves to whatever is hot or popular at that moment. I call it the copycat generation. There is no individuality. People are lost because they don't know who they are and more importantly who God called them to be. You have to find YOU!

The Bible tells us in Roman 12:2, "Be not conformed to this world: but be transformed by the renewing of your mind that you may prove what is good, acceptable, and perfect will of God." God made us unique, and His individual will for each of us is different. We are to be a light in this world. God wants us to be an example of His perfect will. My favorite part of the verse is, "Be transformed by the renewing of your mind." I love this because it's in the transformation process that you will find yourself as your mind is being renewed. God is telling you to stop, take a minute, and just think. When your mind is renewed, you began to start walking in the direction God set for you, not the one you set for yourself. You can start to believe in the vision God gave you—your destiny. You embody it, and everything around you starts to change. Your environment will change, your circle of friends will change, and your vision will become more prominent. As difficult as it may seem, you'll need to spend some time getting to know yourself. It is a necessary step in order to understand your purpose and destiny.

One of the biggest obstacles people face in life is facing the man in the mirror because that man knows the good, bad, and the ugly. We are afraid of the man in the mirror, but I'm here to tell you there is nothing to fear. When you look in the mirror, you'll be liberated, motivated, validated and given the elixir to find yourself. I can remember when I began my transformation. I was broken and lived in discontent. I was trying my hardest to be something I knew I wasn't because it looked good or it seemed fun at the time. I was living this fake made-up life of mine where I looked good on the outside, but I was dying on the inside. I would look at myself some nights and just cry. I didn't believe in myself and certainly didn't believe God could use me. I was out on the streets, messing up to the point that I got kicked out of school. Just like that, I was a high school dropout. There was no reason for me to believe in my dreams when I didn't feel worthy.

Like so many people, I was seeking validation from the world. I made myself believe that since my daddy wasn't there for me, then nobody wanted me. I started reaching for the wrong people, and I came up empty every time. One day after reading Romans 12:2, I came to a conclusion. I wanted my life to change, and that meant I needed a renewed mind if I was going to be who God called me to be. I had to take responsibility to think differently, and that's when it began. I started getting up early every morning. I literally looked in the mirror and spoke life to myself. I would tell myself, "You are the head and not the tail. You are the lender and not the borrower. You are more than a conqueror, and even in your down season, God can still use you." I was battling with low self-esteem, so I had to say these things to myself to build myself back up.

I was careful about monitoring my confessions, only to speak positively and not negatively. I would tell myself, "I am a champion. I am a great leader. I am a man of God, and when I'm down, God's got my back." I would tell myself that I was a millionaire because I had to break the mindset of poverty. I would tell myself, "I love me," fist pound the mirror, and then start my day. The way I validated myself was to quote scriptures like Romans 8:31, "What shall we then say to these things? If God be for us, who can be against us?" I was actively building up my faith.

It says in Romans 10:17, "Faith comes by hearing, and hearing by the word of God." I didn't always have my pastor to read the word to me so I would speak it to myself to build my faith.

I came to the realization that my faith was tied to my destiny. It is not only important to find yourself, but also to believe in the person you find. As I started progressing, I saw a strong man rising and standing up in me. That gang banging boy I told you about was dying. I looked at that man and believed one day this is who I'll be and until that day, I still do. We have been taught to believe in everything but ourselves, like Santa Claus and the Easter bunny. Whom we have never seen—and yet we look in the mirror every day and don't believe in the person we see. How unfortunate is that? I dare you to start believing in that reflection. Don't be like everyone else, changing yourself to fit a lost culture. Create your own culture. You can never be the best copycat in the world, but you can be the best you that God created you to be. I dare you to find your value; I dare you to believe, and I dare you to step out. I dare you to walk into your destiny.

⚲ GOD'S PURPOSE

"The meaning of life is to find your gift. The purpose of life is to give it away." -Pablo Picasso

Sometimes we can be so busy in our lives that we forget there's a purpose behind it. We get caught up with work, in business, in ministry, or for others, it may be marriage. We all get so committed to what we are doing that we forget why we are doing it in the first place. We become slaves to the culture we set for ourselves to live in, not realizing that God has a higher purpose. I can remember when one of my mentors watched me work day in and day out, chasing my dream, literally working my fingers to the bone. One day I recall him asking me, "What my purpose was, and what am I working for?" I really hadn't given it much thought, but now I was intrigued and wanted to figure it out. The first step I took was to research the meaning of purpose and its definition. It is defined as "the reason for which something is done or created or for which something exists." After reading this, I asked myself, *What's my reason? What's my why?* I needed to find out.

A firefighter's purpose is not to put out a fire, it's to save a life. A pastor's purpose is not to preach it's to build the body of Christ, so what was mine? You see, it's so important to find out your purpose because it and destiny work hand in hand. Your destiny is God's destination for you and His purpose is the reason you are even on the road. I believed that by finding myself, I was destined to be great, but why? Steve Jobs once said, "In order to tell the future you have to connect the dots of the past." I can remember at the age of twelve I was looking for work that winter, so I went door to door, asking neighbors to shovel their driveways. Those who allowed me would pay me twenty dollars. My initiative and ambition gave me more yards to shovel than I could handle. It was one cold January afternoon, and I had been working all morning, and my fingers were blistering cold. The moisture from the snow had set in my gloves and socks, and I was freezing. I had three more yards to shovel, but I was cold and dead tired.

On my way home to take a break, I crossed paths with three of my friends. They were out playing, hauling snowballs back and forth. Watching them play, I saw how much energy they had, and that gave me a great idea. I said, "Hey, do you want to make some money?" Of course, they all said yes, so I told them to go grab a shovel and meet me on the corner in about twenty minutes. When they returned, I gave them all an address and told them if the shoveled and did a good job, I would give them each ten dollars. They agreed and went to work. After they finished, I collected my payments from all the houses they did, and I paid them. They were so excited about being paid, they worked with me all winter. I didn't know then, but I had started my first business. It felt good knowing I was instrumental in providing an opportunity to some youth who otherwise didn't have any. In order to find your purpose, you must connect the dots of the past. All the dots may not connect, but the ones that do will truly reveal purpose in your life. I've always been a leader and an entrepreneur. I just had to remember it.

Now that I wanted to help, I needed to know what my why was. I began searching my heart. I found myself looking at the world and what meant the most to me. I wanted to know where I could meet a need. I searched day in and out, asking God to reveal His purpose; then it hit me like a ton of bricks—it was the next generation, the generation the world forgot about, those young guys, the ones full of talent, but waiting for the opportunity to use it. I will be the example to them. I will motivate them, and I will inspire them. I will be the one to give them a chance and expose them to their true talent. To God be the glory! Once I found it, my journey could begin. My destination had been given, and my reason to get on the road was clear.

I believe God has amazing things in store for you, but you have to go after them. Take some time and reflect on your life. Try and remember the one thing you did very well or that job you always wanted as a child. Now align that childhood moment with the adult vision God has deposited into you and find the point of connection. You have to believe God is going to use you. The Bible tells us in 1 Corinthians 2:9, "Eye has not seen, nor ear heard, nor have entered into the heart of man the things which God has prepared for those who love Him," and the same is referenced in (Isaiah 64:4). God is going to do a new thing in you. It's up to you to let Him. I need you to find yourself to accept your destiny. I need you to discover your purpose, and I need you to put that into action. I dare you to stop just working, doing what you are paid for, and begin walking in your purpose doing what you were made for.

"He has saved us and called us to a holy life—not because of anything we have done but because of his own purpose and grace," 2 Timothy 1:9.

CHAPTER TWO

START ROUTE:

Commitment to the PROCESS

"Faith in God is a commitment to start without any guarantee of success."

"One man's obedience is tied into so many people's destiny."
- Pastor John Hannah.

Those words from my pastor echo through my mind and beat on my heart every time I think about giving up. They were so profound that they literally shifted my motivation and focus pertaining to the vision. I mean, there have been nights where I have found myself sitting in a dark room ready to throw in the towel, but those words still play in my mind and remind me of my commitment to the process. *It's bigger than me,* I tell myself. How can I move towards something only I can see, meaning there is no outside proof that it will happen? How can I commit to that? I had to have faith.

The Bible tells us in Hebrews 11:1, "Now faith is the substance of things hoped for, the evidence of things not seen." In order to commit, your faith has to be intact. Look at it this way: when you are planning a trip, you have your start point and your destination. You key that information into a GPS system;

you know that little thing in our cars and on our phones we use when we are lost, and it tells us what to do. That system will calculate the information you punch in and give you a route to follow. Rarely do we question that route, but more so we follow it. We do exactly what the GPS tells us to do. If it says go left, we go left. If it says to go right, we go right. We trust this route the system gives us and believe it will get us to our destination; we commit to the ride.

As Believers, we have to allow God to be our GPS in life, allowing Him to lead us in the right direction. Just like we trust the system, we have to trust the solution, and the solution is God. Just like the GPS system will not inform you when you hit the road that you will get a flat tire or you'll run into a traffic jam, God won't tell you what's on the road ahead; you have to stay focused on the destination you keyed in. What does "keying in" mean? Just like we ask the GPS for directions, when you pray, you ask God for directions. He hears you. All you have to do is believe and step out. "For I know the plans I have for you," declares the Lord, "plans to prosper you and not to harm you, plans to give you hope and a future," Jeremiah 29:11.

♀ STEP OUT
"You make the first step to the rest of your life." - Malcolm Brown

I believed when I tapped into my inner artist and finally used my talent to start a business, that was the route God used to expose me to destiny. But, I didn't know stepping out would be so hard. You would think that when you put God in it, things would go easy or everything would just fall into place.

But contrary to popular belief, that's not how it goes. I'll never forget when my faith was tested in my humble beginnings of building my brand and business. I'll take you back about eight years ago, to the beginning. It was summertime, and I was running new promotions to build clientele, trying out new and creative ways to gain business. I started promoting $100 tattoo parties. Now for those who don't know what a tattoo party is, let me explain. This is when instead of coming to me for service, I would bring the service to you. Genius right?! I know, I know. I thought of it myself, not really. I'm only joking! This was actually something a beginner artist would do to promote themselves. It is the same concept that rap artists use when they book at "hole in the wall" joints. They are not too particular because the purpose is to get exposure for their music. I decided to do the same thing to get some exposure.

I promoted this way for several months. No one called, and I mean no one, but I didn't allow discouragement to stop me from promoting. So one day I finally get a call from a girl I went to high school with. She was having a coming home party for her brother; I believe he was being released from jail. She said there would be a lot of people, and they wanted me to come out. I jumped on it fast because it looked like a good opportunity. At the same time, I could make some money and get my name out there, so I said yes because I was ready to step out. I scrapped up as much money as I could by begging family and friends so I could purchase all new supplies for the party. I purchased everything I needed and the day arrived for me to go out and work. Up until that day I was only saying that this was what I wanted to do, and it felt good now that I was actually doing it. I had taken the plunge and stepped out.

I wasn't at the party very long before things started to get a little funny and uncomfortable. I drove up to this address on the southeast side of Chicago in this rundown neighborhood; the building looked abandoned. The party was in the only unit that was occupied. I noticed while walking down the hallway leading to the apartment that it reeked of urine and weed smoke. I didn't let it phase me because I was stepping out. I started setting up as soon as I got inside the apartment. The living room was full of people, and everyone was waiting for me. So despite the environment, I felt good. This was the first time I was making some progress, and I thought this thing could really work. As far as I was concerned, all that people had said was impossible was now happening. God was allowing me to see it because I chose to step out.

Now I worked the party until about two in the morning. The night was winding down, and it was about time for me to leave. My mom had called and said she was on her way to pick me up. The young lady who invited me out to do the party walked up to me and said she'd be right back. She was going to the store and asked if I needed anything, to give her a call. When I started packing my stuff, I could see a group of guys in the corner out the side of my eye, talking. One of the guys then approached me and asked if I could do one more tattoo for his girlfriend. I said, "Ok, cool." I went to the bathroom, and while I was in there, I put all the money I made that night in my boot. The way things were beginning to transpire didn't sit well with me. I went back and started on the tattoo. It was a simple name, "Max." I drew the design out, and the girl loved it, so I tattooed it.

Even though I was doing the tattoo, I was aware of the guys who were still engaged in a conversation. Suddenly my phone rang, and it was my mom. She was downstairs waiting for me. I told her I had to finish one more, and I would be down shortly. She told me she was going to send my brother to help me pack up. As my brother walked into the apartment, I was wrapping up the young lady's tattoo. She let me know that she loved it and wanted to show her boyfriend. She walked over to the corner where the guys were and showed it to him. I noticed they were having a heated exchange of words, then he walked over to me and said he didn't like it and demanded me to fix it. As this was going on, my brother was packing my stuff, and we were getting ready to head out. I told the guy I couldn't do anything more to it. Although she approved it, I let him know I'd give him back the money.

I was just trying to avoid any problems. I reached into my pocket to give him the money, and he got really hostile and slapped the money out of my hands. Once again, he said, "You're going to fix it." Now the energy in the room had shifted, and the air was thick. Some other guest at the party stood in between us and put that guy and his friends out. My brother and I gathered my things to walk out of the door. Before I knew it, the same guy who started the trouble was standing there. He threw a punch and hit me in my face. Instead of helping us, some people from inside the party grabbed my brother and me. They pushed us into a hallway with about ten guys and locked the door. The next thing that happened was quite brutal; they began punching and kicking us from all directions. My bags dropped, and I hit the ground. All I can remember was telling my brother, "Let's go! Let's go!"

One guy was trying to go in my pockets, and the other was trying to take me out of my shirt. Another guy kicked me in my head, and I almost lost consciousness. Everything seemed to slow down, and I was praying for the Lord to help us. Suddenly, my brother got out from under the crowd and pulled me out by my leg. We both ran out of the building and jumped in my mom's car and yelled, "Drive." My mother never put the car in park, so she was able to pull off fast. There were gunshots in the background, but none of them hit the car. I was sitting in the back-seat, weeping because I couldn't believe what had just happened—I was set up. I never expected such craziness when I decided to step out. A few days had gone by, and I was still sitting in my room. I received a lot of calls to do some work. I lost my tattoo equipment at the party. I was also scared that one of the callers could be one of those guys who attacked us at the party. I was willing to quit before going through that again. I was hurt and depressed, needless to say, but something in me wouldn't let me walk away.

Because I was looking for encouragement, I started reading the Bible and came across Matthew 14:22-33, the account of Jesus walking on water. In this particular passage of scripture, Jesus sent His disciples out on a boat as He went into the mountain to pray. Later that night a storm came, and the wind and waves began to shake the boat. Shortly afterward, Jesus started to walk on the water towards the disciples. As soon as they saw this, they became frightened, not understanding what they were seeing. Then Jesus called out to them and told His disciples not to be afraid. Peter then responded, asking Jesus if it was Him to tell him to come to Him. Jesus told Peter to come, so Peter stepped out of the boat into the water and began to walk towards Jesus. After he saw the wind and waves, he got scared and began to sink. He cried out for Jesus to save him. Immediately, Jesus reached out His hand and caught Peter and put him back in the boat.

As I was reading, I came to the realization that just because God sent you on this journey, doesn't mean it's going to be perfect. It's going to require some work, faith, and focus. You can't be distracted by the storm. Just like the disciples, I was sent out, headed toward a destination. I can only imagine for them the trip was easy until the storm came later that night. You see, that's how it happens in life. One minute everything is fine, and suddenly we get hit by a storm. We find ourselves experiencing debt, sickness, loss—all kinds of unexpected events happen. It is during this time that we must remain strong in our faith. Because through it all, God will still allow you to do something amazing in the midst of the storm just because you stepped out. Just like Peter walking on water, God will allow you to walk on top of what took others down in order to prove that with Him nothing is impossible. The very thing that was supposed to kill you, He will allow you to walk all over it, and each step you take becomes a testament of your faith. Even though I wanted to quit, I had got distracted by the storm that hit me also. I was starting to sink, but I believe it was faith and motivation that got me back up once I realized that it is bigger than me. Whenever I reflect back, I am glad that I did not quit that day. I would never be the man I am today. Needless to say, the storm was necessary. It allowed me to see that God was in the midst of the storm.

Stepping out is one of the most important parts of the process. It is an example of your faith and commitment. Don't give up. In the event you start to sink, call out to Jesus and He will pull you back up. If you are in a situation and you feel your storm has gotten out of control, I want you to pray this prayer,

> *"Lord, today I am calling out to You. Let Your presence be known here and now in this storm. I have started to sink, and only You can pull me back up. I reach my hand out to You, oh Lord. Thank you for reaching back. Amen."*

Once you pray this prayer, you'll immediately begin to see your situation change. Then get back on your square because there is a long road ahead, but if you keep your eyes on the Lord, you can make it. Remember, one man's obedience is tied into so many people's destiny.

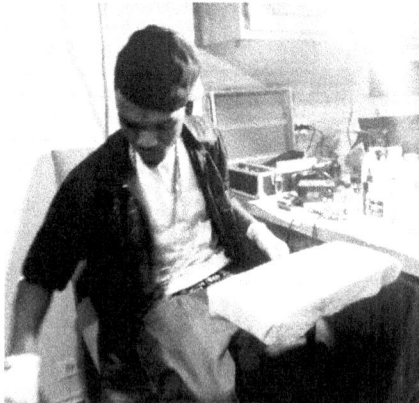

CHAPTER THREE

MOVING THROUGH TRAFFIC:

SEPARATION

"Eagles don't fly with pigeons." - Pastor John Hannah

I remember a certain summer day last year. I was leaving work in University Park, heading to Chicago for a special event one of my mentors invited me to. I merged onto the highway and began my journey. I was moving through traffic, looking for openings between cars to switch lanes and drive faster. I was making good time; then suddenly without warning, I slammed on the brakes. That was my instinctive reaction to this car that jumped in front of me without putting on their signals. I was so livid that I realized it was necessary for me to calm down so I could focus on the trip ahead. This driver not only jumped in front of me on a crowded highway but decided they would drive below the speed limit. I couldn't help but think, *Lord, I'm going to be late now.*

I noticed we had engaged in this slow bumper to bumper song and dance for about a mile. I saw an opening to my left, and I began to merge over into the other lane. Guess who followed? Yes, the slow-moving driver. "I can't catch a break," I yelled out in utter frustration. I remember thinking, *Whoever this person is they have made it their business to irritate the life out of me.* So I went on driving another half a mile then something amazing happened. My prayers were answered, and I spotted an opening. I started merging over to the right, but I didn't even signal because I didn't want the slow mover to catch on to what I was about to do. The car to my right drove past, and there it was. I hit the gas quickly and shot over into the other lane and sped away. I felt so much relief. For a moment I thought I was gonna be late, but I finally made my way past that slow driver. As I continued my trip, I remember jokingly asking God, "Why would you let that person get in front of me?" The response came in a sudden small whisper in my mind that said, "This is your life."

⚲ SEPARATION
"In order to be successful, you must create degrees of separation." - Malcolm Brown

Just like that slow-moving driver, we all have people in our life that are slow-moving and stagnant. There is that person or persons that are literally slowing you down in life. It may be a family member, a significant other, or coworkers. They don't want to do anything, and yet, they want to live off of you. I don't mean to be so frank, but these people exist, and in order to make it to your destiny, you have to separate from them. One of the hardest obstacles to face in life is letting go. You see, when God begins to elevate you, you'll go through a season of separation. You'll begin to see your circle get smaller and smaller, even people you have been in a relationship with for years. God will begin to cut those ties. Don't interfere, just allow it to happen. The Bible tells us in 2 Corinthians 6:17, "Therefore, come out from them and be separate, says the Lord." It was tough for me also, but it was a battle I had to fight and a fight it was.

I shared an eight-year relationship with a young woman. She was someone I truly believed I would be with forever, and I

TEN MILES TO YOUR DESTINY

found myself having to walk away. It started when I was 18, and we met at a military school. We would write letters back and forth to each other, and soon after we left the program, we began dating. We were both from Chicago, but my mother had moved to the suburbs after I graduated. I would travel on the train and get rides to see her as much as I could. It was the perfect nontraditional high school love story. I classify it as nontraditional because we had both dropped out of high school. Although we had both messed up, we were going to tackle the world and build an amazing life together. Initially, we believed we were the perfect match. As the years went by, I started my tattoo business, and she would work odd jobs here and there, and still, we were holding on to this dream. After about the fourth year, I started to feel we were not progressing together. I would sit and have talks with her and asked what she really wanted to do. My business at this point was taking off. I was making good money and was happy, and I wanted the same for her.

I started sensing an extreme lack of motivation on her part. Here I was on fire, chasing the business, and she was just chilling. Conversation after conversation we would talk about her, and she would say things like I want to go to school or I want to work an office job, but never really made any progress in either area. I can understand when you are young that you may not be crystal clear about what you want to do, but to not have a desire to find it was different. We didn't have anything in our way. We had no children and no major setbacks. We were literally living in the realm to explore opportunities. So this continued for several years. The conversations turned into arguments, and because of offense, those conversations turned into breakups. We were in this cycle of destruction. I remember sitting and asking myself why it wasn't working. I came to the realization that we didn't want the same things, and we weren't on the same page. I wanted to live this elaborate life, and she was cool with the average.

I believed in this vision God had given me, but she didn't believe, and as we went on, it started to show more and more. How did we get here? The Bible says, "How can two walk together unless they agree?" I was trying to move in one direction, and she was going in another. I started to change the way I dressed, stopped going out, attended church more, and I was focused on building the business. Before I knew it, I had become a guy she didn't recognize. She wasn't even sure if she liked the new me. Because I loved her, a battle ensued within me, and I found myself going back and forth between who God was calling me to be and being someone opposite of that to please her. Eventually, I realized that if I was truly going to get everything God had for me I would have to leave. That was a struggle because it didn't happen overnight. I was waiting for her to get it.

"Let's grow together," I would always say to her, but it never quite sunk in, and naturally, we grew apart emotionally. Don't get me wrong. I'm not bashing her or the relationship. What I really want you to see is that love doesn't always win. You can both just be moving at different paces and in different directions. Does this sound familiar to anyone? There are going to be people in life that will not understand the vision God has given you, and despite their unbelief, you have to continue moving forward. What makes this story so special is that it's so common. There's a lot of relationships today just like this one where the counterpart is deadweight, and oftentimes the two stay together, and the dream eventually dies. Realize that you mean more and your dreams mean more. You must PUSH PASS IT. Now I'm not telling anyone to leave their spouse but consider yourself and make the necessary space so God's will can be done and He can get the glory out of your life.

On this road we call life, we may experience the holdups of the slow movers in our lives if they are not removed. There is still another to look out for on this road, and I call him or her the reckless driver. There is always that one person or persons on the road driving like they have lost their mind. This person is moving through traffic recklessly, not signaling, speeding, and making sudden stops, ultimately putting everyone driving around them at risk. I'm sure we all know someone like this. At any given moment they can snap, crackle, and pop. It may be someone close to you, and if you are not careful that relationship can be dangerous. The Bible tells us in Proverbs 13:20, "He who walks with wise men will be wise, but the companion of fools will suffer harm." I have a childhood friend who played basketball, and he was amazing. I remember us playing pick up games at the gym, but no one there could hold a candle to this boy. His talent was one of a kind, and his passion was like fire. He went on to play in high school and ended up mixing with the wrong people. This crowd was gang affiliated and included drug dealers. He started hanging out with them more often until his face became familiar.

One day while walking from the park district where we often played ball, my friend and another childhood friend of ours were gunned down by a rival gang member in retaliation to an earlier attack on one of their members. They were shot multiple times, and bullets rattled their bodies. One was hit 18 times and the other 22 times. By God's grace and mercy, they both survived, but both live with lifetime disabilities. Everything he worked for, everything he believed in, his passion and talent were all taken away within a split second because he was associated with the wrong people.

When God has called you to something greater and blessed you with talents and gifts, you have to be very selective about who you spend your time with. You must remember we have an adversary that we must fight each and every day. That adversary is the devil who comes to kill, steal, and destroy. He will use your family and your friends to throw you off and try to rob you of all the promises of God. Be sure to keep your circle tight. The Bible talks about the man who stays away from bad company in Psalm 1:1-4.

"How blessed is the man who does not walk in the counsel of the wicked, nor stand in the path of sinners, nor sit in the seat of scoffers! But his delight is in the law of the LORD, and in His law he meditates day and night. He will be like a tree firmly planted by streams of water, which yields its fruit in its season; and its leaf does not wither; and in whatever he does, he prospers." God wants to elevate you, and in order for you to be elevated, you'll have to begin to create that space.

Begin to pray that God releases those people in your life that have any type of negative influence on you, and when He starts to release them, let them go. You can never move to the next level in your walk unless you release. Submit to the process and allow God to work in your life. Allow Him to change your environment from the inside out. Don't be afraid to let go of people. What if God is saying to release them because He has someone bigger for you, someone better— better relationships, better friends, better coworkers, or a better lifestyle. It's ok to be a little afraid because change is different; it's difficult, but it's necessary. Maybe there's someone's name that's beating on your chest, and you know God is asking you to let go. Will today be your day? Begin to pray and ask God to remove them out of your life, surrender them to Him, and let the separation begin. I'm standing with you every day, fighting to let go of the old and welcome in the new, so just know you're not alone. I'm excited about your future whoever you are; I love you and God Bless.

CHAPTER FOUR

SPEEDING:

Proceed with CAUTION

What do you do when you are blessed? Everything is going right, your business is in order, you have been promoted on the job, you have money in the bank, and it seems like everything is perfect. God has blessed you with a season of fast progression. It's similar to a cool night on the road, and there is no traffic. There is no one on the road but you, and no one is watching, and you have the opportunity to drive a little over the speed limit. God has allowed you to move or elevate quickly. What it took others to do in ten years, God has allowed you to do in just one. Where others have struggled, you have not. You are continually being blessed and moving forward. What do you do? That answer is to proceed with caution.

I've been working in my industry for seven years now, and my business has been open for half that time. I grew in my industry extremely fast—it was almost overnight. I can remember having to take a step back just to look at what God had allowed me to do in a short period of time, and I was floored. I had one of the largest clienteles in my city, and I was bringing in a six-figure income. I was enjoying these blessings without having a permanent location. So I decided to open a business and began searching for a location. It didn't take long before I found my place and started the leasing process. After I received my copy of the lease to review, I scheduled an appointment to consult with my pastor. I kept my appointment with him. We sat in his office and talked for a while about a number of things, but there were two major things he told me before we prayed over my lease and wrapped up our appointment. Those two lessons will stick with me forever. He told me that the favor of God was on my life, and I was blessed. He said God was about to enlarge my territory, but there were two things I needed to know. The first thing he told me was to maintain my position and the second was to be aware of these three vices; they were money, woman, and pride. What was he telling me?

⊙ MAINTAIN YOUR POSITION
"Stay right there."

The Bible tells us in Luke 12:48, "For unto whomsoever much is given, of him much shall be required." He was letting me know that the same things I've done to get where I was, I would have to do that and more to maintain the blessings of God. You see, God wants to bless His people and He tells us in Jeremiah 29:11, "For I know the plans I have for you declares the Lord, plans to prosper you and not harm you, plans to give you hope and a future." But can He trust you with it? Could He trust me?

The same fire, the same drive that I had to go after God and my destiny, I would have to increase it. There are times in your spiritual walk and in business when elevation or success can cripple you. It can infect you with a condition called *comfortability*. You can never grow too comfortable with God or our destiny. You have to be like David in Psalms 42:1, "As the deer pants after the water brooks, so pants my soul after you, O God," in order to go to a new level of worship. You've worked this hard to go higher with God, so you can't fall off. It's almost like planting a seed. You've watered that seed, gave it sunlight, and pulled all the weeds from around it. Once the first leaves sprout, you sit back and chill. No, this is the time when you have to turn it up a notch.

You have to take your prayer to the next level, your worship to the next level, and your physical walk. You have to take your work ethic to the next level, and then you'll have to grind. God wants to take you from glory to glory according to 2 Corinthians 3:18, so you must continue to climb and continue to work, you must not get comfortable.

⚲ MONEY

"You can't serve two masters."

"For the love of money, is a root of all kinds of evil" 1 Timothy 6:10 (NIV).

Some people, eager for money, have wandered from the faith and pierced themselves with many griefs. There are many people in the world today that have been blessed with financial success, and it can be seen every day on platforms like social media. You can literally google one million dollars, and a picture will pop up on the screen of one million dollars in cash, and because of this, people today desire money more. In this present day, money can give you status, and people are being glorified for their financial status. The lavish lifestyles of the rich and famous with their cars and the jewelry have people more concerned about the material things than the spiritual things. The more begin to go after stuff and financial gain, the further you'll fall away from God and ultimately abort the promise, your destiny. You see, when you fall in love with money, it'll have you doing all kinds of things, and this is what my pastor was warning me about.

There is a man in the Bible by the name of Judas. He was one of Jesus' twelve disciples, handpicked by Jesus Himself. The scripture describes in Matthew 10 how he is also the one Jesus chose to keep the money. The Bible tells us in John 12:6 that he was stealing the money, and as we can see, he had a strong love for money. Jesus chose him to be a part of His ministry team. He was given the power to heal and trusted to oversee the money to take care of them, and yet he was stealing. This shows he was motivated by money. For some people today, money means so much, they are willing to do anything to get it. So later on in the Bible, when the chief priest and the other officers were looking for a way to get rid of Jesus, let's see who came forward. The Bible records in Luke 22:4-5, "And Judas went to the chief priests and the officers of the temple guard and discussed with them how he might betray Jesus. They were delighted and agreed to give him money." How can you fall so in love with money to the point where it becomes a curse? Money is literally supposed to be a seed, but your love for it has turned it into a tool for the devil to use and eventually it will cause you to lose everything.

As you read Luke 22:47-54, it describes how the love of money caused Judas to betray Jesus, and He was taken captive. All it took was 30 pieces of silver. After realizing what he had done, Judas began to feel remorseful and tried to return the money as described in Matthew 27:1-5, but he later committed suicide. You have to be careful that you are not walking through life looking for the next come up or moving out of financial gain. Many people go into business looking only at the monetary gain of doing deals with people because there is big money on the line. Some people run after titles and positions on jobs that don't go with the call that's on their life. The money may fill your pocket, but it will not serve your soul, and you'll feel a void in your heart because it'll never be enough. God is and will forever be all you need. Be careful you're not moving forward on "opportunities" just because it looks like you'll make a lot of money. Because you could be committing suicide in the spirit, and ultimately it can cost you what you didn't expect, your destiny.

♥ WOMEN/MEN
"Guard Your Anointing"

This is what I believe to be one of the most important lessons my pastor taught me that day we had our sit down. He said to watch out for those women; I remember laughing to myself because when he said it, he had this silly look of concern on his face. I was thinking to myself, *They can't be that bad.* Even though I chuckled, I really believe that statement was very profound. I came to realize later after bumping my head with exactly what he said; some people are not attracted to you, but more so they are attracted to the anointing and favor that is on your life. This goes for both men and women. There are some who have been truly blessed by God. His hand is on your life, and you are walking in His glory. What happens is people see that, and then they run to it. They are like flies to a zap trap. You must be on guard with these people because they are literally on assignment to throw you off of what God called you to do or even test your relationship with God.

I remember reading in Genesis 39 where it talks about a young man named Joseph, who was known as "the dreamer." Here is a little background about Joseph and his family. He was despised by his brothers, and eventually, they sold him into slavery, but God was with him. The Bible tells us after Joseph was sold to the Ishmaelites, he was taken down to Egypt and Potiphar, an officer of Pharaoh, bought him. The Lord was with Joseph and allowed him to have success. As a result of his success, Potiphar put Joseph in charge of all of his business. Potiphar did not worry himself with the dealings of Joseph concerning his household; he trusted Joseph because God caused his success. The Lord caused Potiphar's house to prosper because of the anointing and favor that was upon Joseph. Potiphar's wife had become attracted to Joseph, and the Bible says in Genesis 39:7, "And it came to pass after these things, that his master's wife cast her eyes upon Joseph, and she said, 'Sleep with me.'" She wanted what was on him, not just him, even though the Bible describes him as handsome. I believe that she was also attracted to the power and authority given to him by God.

As the story goes on, starting in Genesis 39:9, Joseph said to her, "There is no one greater in this house than I, nor has he kept back anything from me but you, because you are his wife. How then can I do this great wickedness, and sin against God." Joseph knew that all of his power, possessions, and favor came from God, and he was unwilling to sin against his God. At that very moment, he knew he had to protect his anointing! He knew that sleeping with her would drain virtue from him and drive a wedge between the relationship he had with God. She tried everything she could to get Joseph to sleep with her. Don't you just hate when a person keeps pressing the issue after you have already made it clear you don't want to have anything to do with them? It got so bad, the Bible tells us, that one time when Joseph went into the house to do his work, while no one else was there, she grabbed him by his garment and said, "Sleep with me." If that isn't the devil, I don't know what is! But the Bible tells us that Joseph left his garment and ran outside. So his master's wife became angry, and she lied on Joseph, saying he had tried to sleep with her to mock her. The garment she grabbed from Joseph was used to support and prove her lie. Later he was thrown in jail.

This is a sad story because as we read it, he was lied on and taken to jail for something he didn't do. Wisdom would have said that after the person has exposed themselves, to stay as far away from them as possible. The following scripture gives us wisdom concerning compromising situations, 1 Thessalonians 5:22-23, "Abstain from every form of evil. Now may the God of peace Himself sanctify you completely; and may your whole spirit, soul and body be preserved blameless at the coming of our Lord Jesus Christ." It is easier to defend yourself if you are not remotely putting yourself in a compromising situation. Yes, Joseph was in charge of taking care of the house, and he had to go in to do his work, BUT Potiphar's wife had come to him once before saying, "Sleep with me." He was already made aware of her intentions and yet, he still allowed her to get close enough to him to remove his garment.

You WILL run into many people who are attracted to the God in you because they will see your light. They may watch you from a distance, and some may even get bold enough to confront you by saying, "Let's go out," or "Can I get to know you?" It doesn't have to mean they want to get involved sexually. It may simply mean to get to know you or to get involved with you. It is easier to run in some cases, and in others, it's not. Sometimes Satan will send things and people who will grab our attention. He will use something to attract us to our old lives and even our natural senses, but believe me, nothing about this type of encounter is spiritual. We don't fully intend to get close to that thing or person, but we linger just long enough for the "accuser" (Satan) to make a case against us. In some cases, we are simply ministering to them, and then we get close and create a fellowship. Even in ministry, we have to guard our anointing because others are always watching, especially Satan. Sometimes we are fully aware of the intentions of the person, whether it's good or bad, but in some cases we are blind, and that's why it is so critical to guard your anointing by any means necessary and at all times.

The devil is out to steal, kill, and destroy. He knows your place in the kingdom, and he will send things and people your way to try to knock you off track and steal your promise. Sometimes, like Joseph, we may come to our senses and sometimes we may not. How many times have you thought that you had a situation "under control." Before you know it, you end up doing something that you regret. It simply happened because you allowed things to go too far with someone that you had no business being with in the first place. You decided that it was alright. And how many times in those situations did your relationship with God begin to change? You weren't praying as you should, going to church as much, and not reading the Word at all. You did not protect your anointing.

For someone reading this, it's time to get out of there! Guard your anointing! It's time to get it right and get back to doing the right things. No more lying around with any and every one. The devil is after your anointing—get on point. Don't believe the hype, those demons are on assignment to come rob you of your destiny.

♀ PRIDE
"The Bigger You Are the Harder You Will Fall."

"BE HUMBLE AND SIT DOWN!" I'm gonna pause on the Bible references and hold off on the scriptures for this part; I want us to sit back and just have some real talk. Pride is something I believe we all struggle with. Life and success can really put you in a place to where the old folks would say, "You start smelling yourself," and the more you ignore it, the more it grows. Some of you might say, "I don't struggle in this area," but we all know we do. No? Ok, well I'll just speak for myself. On my journey, I've had a season where pride had gotten ahold of me, and it was not letting go. The business had started to get better for me, and I was really growing quickly. My social media following had grown to almost 10k people overnight, and my name was being praised. I had met a man named Leroy, and he began to work with me, building a street team to move my flyer throughout the city of Chicago, so my work was everywhere.

Things were going so well that I was doing 12 to 15k a month in sales, and the money was flowing in. I had a new location that had great walk-in traffic, and I even purchased a billboard off the major expressway with my face and business name on it. Not too shabby for a 20-year old, right? It was amazing. I mean one minute I'm begging people to come to me, and the next, my phone line was ringing off the hook. I had a real sense of accomplishment looking at everything; I felt like I had arrived and I did it all myself.

Pause, *I did it all myself!*

Let's review the definition of pride. **Pride** - a feeling or deep pleasure or satisfaction derived from one's own achievements, the achievements of those with whom one is closely associated, or from qualities or possessions that are widely admired. I was really lost in myself, and I felt like I was in control. I was making these things happen, and I got so confident I stopped praying, stopped asking for help, and I was turning my nose up at people like I was better than they were. It had gotten so bad, people that when anyone would try to give me advice, I would ignore it because I felt like their opinion did not matter. I knew it all, and you couldn't tell me anything. Needless to say, "I was tripping." That pride was standing up in me strong; then came the fall.

I was driving in my car, leaving the city heading to the suburbs to meet a client. I was running late, so I was driving a little fast. The traffic was thick, and I was rushing, switching lanes back and forth like a madman. I didn't care because I honestly felt as though I was unstoppable. You wouldn't believe what happened next. I was driving around a bend, and I saw a tight opening in the next lane between the car in front of me and the one to my right side. So I put my foot on the gas and darted over to the right lane quickly. Either I was moving too fast, or I didn't time it correctly and the unthinkable happened—my car began to drift out of control. I turned the wheel to the left, clearing the guardrail by the slightest inch, then quickly swerved right, just missing a small car to my left. My car suddenly drove off onto the shoulder of the road. The sound of rocks and pebbles hitting the side of the car was loud, and my vision had become limited because of the dust clouds that formed from my tires sliding in the dirt. I started to feel my car fishtail, so I cut the wheel one more time to the left and hit the gas. My car shot back into oncoming traffic and all I could hear was a loud horn.

At this point, it felt like things slowed down and time was really moving in slow motion. As I was exiting this cloud of dust, I looked over my left shoulder out of the driver-side window, and I was staring at the grill of a semi-truck. I couldn't believe what I was seeing, and a strong feeling of fear came over me. All I could do was grab the wheel and call on the name of Jesus. I heard a loud bang, and things sped up. My body was jerking from left to right and objects from inside the car were flying from all directions. "Please Lord, save me," was my prayer, as this was happening. My car was flipped six times and then went through a fence on an adjacent road off the expressway. When it finally stopped, I could remember still holding the steering wheel and preparing for another hit, but one never came.

I could hear the sound of traffic coming from the busy expressway. As I looked around, I could see broken glass and smoke. There was blood all over my hands and shirt, and my body was stiff. I sat there for about two minutes before realizing the car was on fire. *I had to move quickly,* I remember thinking, but I couldn't seem to move. My mind was telling me to do one thing, but my body wouldn't listen. *Lord, please help me,* was the thought running through my mind. I was stuck in this burning car, wedged in between the door on the driver side and the center console. I just knew I was going to die. One minute I was on top of the world feeling as if I was in control of it all, and then my life was hanging in the balance, and there was nothing I could do. With tears running down my face and still struggling to move, I laid my head back and said, "Lord, if you can hear me, save me," and then I closed my eyes.

Suddenly, I heard the sound of a car door closing and voices saying, "Go to the other side and see if someone's in there." As I opened my eyes, I saw a man waving his hand to clear the smoke. He looked at me, and our eyes connected. What he saw was a boy trembling with fear. "He's alive," he yelled out. "You're going to be ok. Come on this side, hurry we've got to get him out!" He reached in and began to pull me out, instructing the other person to grab my legs. They got me out, carried me to a safe area down the road, and laid me on the ground.

I could remember looking over and seeing the car was engulfed in a huge flame. "Hey, hey, stay with me. What's your name?" the man asked me, and I tried to respond, but I couldn't utter a word. The shock of what had just happened was setting in, and my mind was racing. My hands started to get cold, and my head started to spin, and to make matters worse, my legs were becoming stiff. "He's going into shock. Get an ambulance down here!" he yelled out to his partner, and the man then grabbed me and started to rock back and forth. "Hey, my name is Roy, young man. You're going to be ok. We have an ambulance on the way." He continued to rock me and talk with me until help came. They got me into the ambulance and to the hospital.

The doctors immediately ran into the room and began cleaning me up and running all types of tests. Check this out; all the blood came from a hairline scratch over my eyebrow. All the tests came back clear, and there wasn't a broken bone in my body. Everything was intact. That was God! So later I was discharged to go home. As soon as I got home, I laid down to get some rest, and that's when the Lord began to speak to me. That same night I had a dream, and in this dream was a replay of my accident. I could see something in the car with me, something dark, and my car was attacked by similar dark figures. It was tossed from left to right, and it was almost as if these figures were trying to get to me. They kept coming from all directions, hitting the car, then suddenly, a man with a bright aura of light around him came down out of the sky and stopped my car from flipping. Then another came with full body armor on and grabbed my hand and pulled me out of the car and laid me down. As I looked to my side, lying there, I could see more of these men with this aura of light around them, descending from the sky, and they began to surround me. The dark figures rushed toward me, and they incited a battle like none other, and then I woke up.

Shaken by what I had just seen, I was afraid to go back to sleep because I could not understand what it was about. So I began to pray, and the Lord told me that to the carnal eye, I had a bad car accident, but in the spirit, there was a battle over my life, and it was He who saved me. It was not by luck, and it was not by coincidence, and it was nothing I did, but it was the hand of the Lord that spared my life. I immediately began to repent and ask God to forgive me. I also realized the figure in the car with me was the spirit of pride and arrogance and those other figures were other spirits coming to take me out. That dream helped me understand that when you don't address an evil spirit when it shows up, it will grow, and it will invite more of them to come. Here I thought I was in control and really I was the one under attack. You must be humble on this journey God is taking you on to meet destiny. Understand that everything you have comes from the Lord. It's not your job, your degree, or your intellect—God is your source. Take some time and really evaluate yourself. Be honest and don't be like me. You don't have to have a near-death experience or lose everything to realize you are off. Take the time now and address it. You can ask God for forgiveness and guidance on how to move forward.

CHAPTER FIVE

THE REROUTE:

Making The Wrong TURN

"It's not about the mistakes we make, but how we take correction that defines us."

What do you do when you have made the wrong turn? Have you ever been driving, and you hit a dead zone? Your GPS is on, but you're not paying attention to the reception so the system has stalled and you end up going the wrong way. Driving for miles before you realize you are going in the wrong direction, what do you do? That answer, in my opinion, is simply nothing; you have to stop, sit, and wait. What will end up happening is once the GPS system reconnects, it will recalculate an alternative route for you to follow putting you back on course to your destination. Sometimes in life, we can move too fast and not pay attention. We forget to listen to God's voice, the one that's directing us. We can hear that voice and ignore it, causing a disconnect in the spirit. We will make a mistake and end up going down some roads in life we never thought we would, but if we catch ourselves, stop, and wait on God, He will put us back on track.

The Bible tells us in Psalms 37:23, "The steps of a good man are ordered by the Lord." This means God knows the route for you to take and He knows you will make a mistake, so He already has an alternative route for you. But in order for you to get it, you have to stop and be still. Exodus 14:13, "Don't fear, stand still, and see the salvation of the Lord." There is a blessing in standing still because God is coming to get you. He didn't say there wouldn't be consequences for your mistakes; He just promised that He would get you out. The Lord is going to go before you and set up something on this alternative route. He will provide you with some help, but you still have to go down this road, and it may not be pretty. It's like being in a furnace, and God promises to protect you and get you out. The flames may not hit you, but that doesn't mean you won't feel the heat. So while you wait, you need to reconnect in prayer, and in your worship, because you'll need to hear and see God in the reroute.

HOW DID I GET HERE?

"Hello."

"Where are you?"

"I'm leaving the shop; I'll be there in a minute."

"Ok, hurry up. I'm not waiting for you all night."

"I'm on my way!"

This was the conversation that shifted my entire night. It was a Saturday night, and I was locking up my tattoo shop and heading out to chill with a friend of mine. Now my business brings in a large amount of cash on the weekends so I would carry my firearm during those days to protect my clients, my staff, and myself. My normal routine is for me to lock the door, pull the cash drawer, then pull my safe. After all of that is finished and the money is secure, I would then put my firearm up in its proper case. This night in a scramble to leave, I moved too fast and left with the gun still in the holster on my hip. I got in the car with one of my employees, since he was dropping me off at my destination. As we were driving, I realized I still had the gun on me. I told him that I had it, but we didn't think anything of it. We should have stopped and secured it, but we didn't.

As we got closer to approaching my location, I started to gather my things to exit the car. My plan was to get out and go in the house, but my plan was interrupted when the following happened: As we turned the corner while heading down the block where the house was, we noticed a car just sitting there. As soon as we passed the car, it started to follow us. Once we got to the end of the block where the house was, and we parked, another car then sped around the corner and stopped directly in front of us, cutting us off. Police lights came on from the car behind us and the one in front of us. I heard car doors slam, and all I could see were flashlights and guns pointing towards our car. "Get out of the car!" There were about six police officers dressed in street clothes surrounding our car. They pulled us out and pushed us against the back doors. With guns still pointing directly towards us, they told us if we moved they would blow our heads off.

The officer that grabbed me had begun to search me. He started with my pockets and found the cash I left my shop with. I had six-thousand dollars that were in increments of hundreds, twenties and five-dollar bills. He asked me where I got it, but things were moving so fast I couldn't answer. He then searched my waistband and found my gun. He said, "We got a gun!" and the officers then turned towards me, pointing their guns. My hands went up in the air, and I was put in a chokehold. One officer removed the gun from my waistband, and the officer that had me in the chokehold slammed me to the ground. Another officer then came and put his knee in the back of my neck and held my face to the concrete while the other one handcuffed me. "Do you have anything else on you?" "No!" I yelled, fearing for my life, not knowing what would happen next. I then began explaining to the officer that I was a business owner, and I was traveling home from a night at work. I told him the gun was registered, and I had my Illinois FOID card in my wallet. We went through all the motions, and everything came back cool. One officer told his sergeant that everything checked out, and it was up to him as to what should happen next. I'll never forget how he looked me in my face and said, "You're going to jail."

When I got to the station, I was told I was being charged with a misdemeanor for having the gun out of the case. They told me I would be released in six hours, but after about an hour, all that changed.

"Brown!" said the officer.

"Yeah, that's me," I replied.

"Well, it looks like you're not going home tonight. You're being booked."

"Why?" I asked the officer.

"You're being charged with a felony. You have court in the morning. Do you need to make a phone call?"

The room began to spin, my palms started to sweat, and my knees got weak. I couldn't believe what I just heard.

"What do you mean felony? What felony? I ain't hurt nobody. I was just going home," I told him.

"Aggravated UUW. That gun was loaded, and it had a live

round in it. You broke the law, and you're not going home. Do you need to make a phone call?"

I could tell by the negative energy in the room that he was irritated, and there was no reasoning with him, so I took the phone call.

Ring…ring…ring…you have reached the voicemail box of——

"Hey bro, I tweaked. I got locked up for the pistol. I have to go to court in the morning at the county. Come get me, bro. Come get me."

I hung up the phone and went back to the holding cell and just sat there thinking. The events of the night were replaying in my mind. What could I have done differently? What did I do wrong? I kept asking myself what had happened and how I had gotten there. I was overwhelmed with feelings of anxiety and fear about what was going to happen next. I began to pray and said, "Father if you can hear me, I need you now." As I sat in the cell, a very comforting feeling overcame me. I can't explain it, but somehow I knew in my heart that everything was going to be alright.

♀ DISCONNECTED/*RECONNECTED*

That whole night even before the incident took place, I knew in the back of my mind that I was supposed to lock up my gun. It was routine, and that voice in my head kept saying, "Leave it here. Lock it up," but I didn't listen. While we were driving, we had every opportunity to stop and go back and put the gun back in its proper place, but I didn't, and now I'm here. I was letting my flesh dictate my actions that night instead of listening to my spirit. It amazes me how many of us ignore that voice in our head; you know the one that says, "Go left," and we go right, or the one that says, "Don't," and we do it anyway. This is a constant battle for all of us, the battle between our flesh and our spirit. How many times have you been in a situation when you knew the right thing to do, but you still chose to do what's wrong? For example, you have a verbal altercation with someone, and your spirit man says, "Walk away," but your flesh says to tell them off. You know it's better to take the high road and walk away, but how many of us stay? Ok, maybe it's just me.

In Romans 7:14-25, the Bible tells us about this battle in which a man by the name of Paul is describing the battle he's having with himself. He is having a conversation with himself, and he is basically saying what we all say to ourselves when we mess up. *Dang man!* He's looking at himself, and he's saying, "I want to do what's right, I really do, but this flesh has a hold on me, and I come up short sometimes." He's so upset, he starts to come down on himself like some of us do. He said in Romans 7:24, "O wretched man that I am!" This sounds so familiar, but instead, we say things like, "Man I was tripping," or "Dang, I'm stupid for that," or "It seems like I can't do anything right." We find ourselves dwelling on our mistakes, but just like Paul, you have to find the solution. In Romans 7:25, he confesses that he is grateful to God that through Jesus Christ he could, with his mind, serve the law of God. It's time to reconnect, and we must begin to seek God even in the midst of our mistakes. When I realized I had messed up, I knew it was time for me to pray.

I understood what was ahead of me, but I couldn't get through it by myself. I needed God, and the only way to reconnect was through repentance and prayer.

⚲ GOD, I HEAR YOU

Now that I was released from jail, my best friend and one of my brothers came and posted a bond for me the next morning. My reroute journey had begun. Soon I would have to go to court and fight for my life, so I needed legal representation. I started calling around, looking for lawyers. I called one law office after another and that included the top firms in Chicago down to the shady ones you find on late-night television. Needless to say, I was on a relentless search for the right person; you know this is my life, and I couldn't afford to play with that. To no avail, I came up short. Some of the lawyers had amazing records and were highly accredited, but something about them just wasn't right. They looked good on paper, but they didn't sit right with my spirit and for some reason, we were not connecting. So I began to call on some of my friends and mentors to see if they had anyone in mind. Two lawyers, in particular, came up. My mentor Charles had referred me to a guy named Mr. Allen, and my best friend Kris had referred me to one of his clients named, John F. Lyke. Both of these guys, Kris and Charles have a powerful influence on my life, so after speaking with them, I stopped my search and just focused on the references they gave me. I called both lawyers and set up a meeting.

I met with Mr. Allen first. He was young and sharp; he was building a great career and reputation for himself and most of all, he was concerned about my case. Unlike some of the other law offices I called previously where I was just a case file, he seemed genuinely concerned. He admitted that he didn't want to see a successful young brother go down the drain and get locked into the system. We talked a little more about my situation, and then he gave me his price, which was a $2,500 retainer. That was doable, and I told him I would take what we discussed under consideration and reach out if I needed him. The next meeting I set up was with John Lyke. When I met with John, it was like meeting Kobe. I walked into his office in Hyde Park, Chicago, and he had a full staff. He was taking calls left and right. I mean things were really shaking and moving around there, and he was in the center of it all. He called me into his office, and we sat down. From the tone in the office, I knew I wasn't messing with a guy that didn't mean business. He had an amazing track record, and besides that, he had played on both sides of the fence, prosecutor and defense. I'm not going to say that he was old. I'll just say he was more seasoned and put together. Nevertheless, we spoke about my case and what was so amazing to me was after a short conversation with minimum details about what had happened that night, *he* told *me* everything that had happened that night; sounds crazy right? He also showed the same concern about my wellbeing and me winning this case. He informed me that he was going to do everything he could to win my case.

So, after talking a little bit more with him, he quoted me a price of $5,000, double what Mr. Allen would charge me. He required me to pay half of that amount up front in order to take the case. In the back of my mind, I said, *Dang, that's going to hurt, but it's doable.* We shook hands, and I told him I'd call him if I needed him. Now that I met these guys, they both seem to be great lawyers, and the court date was approaching. What would I do? I prayed and asked God, "Who do you want me to go with? You tell me, and I won't move until I hear from you." My court date was two days away, and God hadn't said anything. I was looking at my bank account, and there wasn't a lot of money in there. I needed to make a decision, so I called the more affordable lawyer, Mr. Allen. I give him the date and time and which courtroom we would be in, and he said, "Ok." Almost immediately, I received a call from John Lyke.

He said, "Hey young man, you have court in two days. Will I see you there?"

A little embarrassed to say, I responded, "Well sir, I ended up going with someone else."

He replied, "Ok that's fine, who by the way?"

"Mr. Allen."

He said, "Ok, call me if you need me."

After that, I just sat thinking, "Why did he call me, especially after I just told the other lawyer he got the case?"

I started wondering if God was trying to tell me something. The first day I didn't think anything of it, but the closer we got to my court date, it was beating on my chest to call John back and put him on the case. What was that beating I felt on my chest? I believe it was the answer I was waiting on, that voice in my head, you know, God's voice. If ignoring it was how I got into this situation in the first place, listening to it was how I was about to get out. "God, I hear you loud and clear!" That Monday morning, I got up, got ready, and headed to court. I called Mr. Allen, and I told him, "I apologize, but I don't need your services today. I decided to go with someone else." I went inside the court building and waited outside the courtroom where my case was going to be heard, and I prayed, "God, if this is Your will, please make a way." I called John Lyke.

Ring...ring...ring....

"You have reached Attorney John Fitzgerald Lyke Jr. I'm not able to answer the phone right now. Please leave a message." I left this message on his machine: "Hi, Attorney Lyke. This is Malcolm. I know I told you I didn't need your services, but if you could—" Beep.

I looked, and as I was leaving the message, John was calling on the other line. I quickly answered.

"Hello." What he said next was music to my ears.

"Hey Malcolm, what's up my man. You called me?"

"Yes sir, I did, and I'm at court and it starts in about 30 minutes. I know that I told you that I didn't need your services, but I believe God said for me to call you. Please if you can help me." "What courtroom are you in?"

I told him the room number, and I'll never forget what he said next.

"God told me to call you back. I'm in the next room and I'll see you in a minute."

After a year of fighting this case, we won with a not guilty ruling. John Lyke later went on and became a judge, and I was his last case before he was sworn in to take the bench. Also, he is now my mentor. As you go through your reroute, and as you pray, being keen to hearing God's voice, He will give you guidance, and you will find your way out. God is going to have you take calculated steps and set you up with some divine connections, but your ears have to be open to listening. Don't keep making the same mistakes like I was about to, moving too fast and not waiting on God. Be still and listen, He'll tell you just what to do.

📍 GOD, I KNOW IT'S DARK, BUT I CAN SEE YOU

What is seeing God? Activating your faith. How do you do that? Let me explain. There will be some moments on this reroute that will not be very pretty. You might have to go through some tough situations and some hard times, but always remember that God is with you and is fighting for you. Like I said earlier, you may find yourself locked in this furnace, and the only way out is through. God is going to direct you, and He will protect you. The flames will not hit you, and you will not die in this thing, but while you are in there, you will feel the heat. Don't let that get you off course; the heat is just a distraction. You have to be able to see God in the midst of it all. I had some tough moments while fighting this case when I thought it was over for me and I was done. I was feeling the heat, but God reminded me that He was with me.

There was one moment I remember like it was just yesterday. We were in pretrial reviewing the case. Leading up to this point, there were a number of things that had already transpired. If I could paint a picture of the temperature in the courtroom, it was hot. Prior to this date, the officers had lied in their statement saying that I had yelled out that I had a gun. Their reason for stopping us was illegal, but they stated that it was because we were parked twelve inches off the curb, which was nonsense, and a host of other things that didn't add up. So, as you can kind of see, at this point, things are not going as planned and the heat is real. On this date, our plan was to put in a motion to suppress evidence. In essence, that means the prosecutor would not be able to use the evidence against us in trial based on the fact that it was found illegally. Ok, so we preceded with this and presented our case. We mentioned the bogus stop, the illegal search, and we also mentioned the fact that all the testimonies given by the police were inconsistent. With no regard, the judge looked at us and denied our motion and set a trial date.

As we were leaving the courtroom, I looked at John Lyke and asked, "What is going to happen next?" and "What is the worst that could happen?" He said, "What happens next is we keep fighting this, and the worst that could happen is you'll go

TEN MILES TO YOUR DESTINY

to jail." When he said that my heart stopped, up until that moment that didn't even seem real. Initially, I had no doubt that I'd be fine until I heard those words and then things got real. Seeing the expression on my face, he knew I needed to be comforted, so he assured me that everything was going to be alright, and that's what I hired him for. In my mind, I was thinking, Yeah, right. You are about to get me locked up. As I left the courthouse and was driving home, all I could think of was the judge saying, "Motion denied." Over and over again it played in my head, and every time I got a little more uncomfortable and scared. What are my next steps? What's going to happen to my business? What's going to happen to me? I'm not ready for this; I'm not prepared. I haven't hurt anyone. Why me? Yes, I was in that car, losing my mind, but suddenly something amazing happened—I activated my faith.

I had to remember the same God that saved me from a car accident was going to save me from this. The same God that protected me when I got jumped and robbed was going to cover me through this. The same God that was leading me through this was going to get me out. I had to remember and not forget all that God had done for me. The Bible tells us in Hebrews 13:8, "That Jesus Christ *is* the same yesterday, today, and forever." So if He did it then, He was going to do it again. I had to encourage myself and believe God was up to something. About a month later, our trial date came and instead of a jury trial, we choose a bench trial. What a bench trial consists of is me, my lawyer, the judge, and the prosecutor. Both parties would argue their case again, and the evidence would be presented. On my way to court, I was getting more and more nervous. I was quite aware that this could be the day everything changed for me. After I arrived and parked, I sat in my car and began to pray. "Spirit of the living God, let Your presence be known in this courthouse today, fill the room with Your glory, get the victory on today God, in Jesus' name.

Amen." After praying, I got out of the car and walked to the building with confidence, knowing that God was with me. I even recited what David told Goliath before their battle. "You come against me with sword and spear and javelin, but I come against you in the name of the LORD Almighty, this day the LORD will deliver you into my hands, and I'll strike you down." I was activating my faith and speaking to the giant I was facing.

When I walked in, I felt the tone in the courtroom was different, and I knew God was up to something. We started our court proceeding. The prosecution went first, presenting what evidence they had and then read the police statements. On paper, I was a young black boy in the hood with a gun on a Saturday night standing against a 16-year veteran Chicago police officer. He had a reputation of taking guns off the streets and collared felons every day. My defense team presented the illegal stop and search, and it all came down to my word against his. It was obvious they would need some more hard evidence to book me. The judge then asked about the gun. The prosecutor looked and looked, then suddenly their team was scrambling. One whispered to the other, and they addressed the judge. "Your honor, we don't have a weapon." The judge then replied, "Explain." Another prosecutor then stepped up and said, "When we went to pull it from evidence, we were told it was not in CPD's custody." The judge looks at me, then looks at them and said, "Well, if you don't have a gun then you don't have a case. Not guilty. Young man, go home."

He hit his gavel and called the next case. Everything had happened so fast. I was shocked. I looked at my lawyer and asked, "What just happened?" He said, "We won," and suggested we get out of there before they change their minds. I got up and walked out of that courtroom; my best friend was there waiting in the hallway. We greeted each other with a hand smack and hugged, celebrating what God had just done. I can't make this up. The people in the lobby started clapping their hands and everything. It was like something out of a movie. Activate your faith, and you will see God in your situation. To this day, we still don't know what happened to that gun, but I believe it was God that delivered me from that case. Not only did He deliver me, but He hooked me up with someone who has exposed me to another world. He gave me a divine connection and placed me in a new circle. When you are able to see God in the midst of your test, it will become your testimony. Your confessions will change. You go from saying, "I wish I never did it," to "Had I not gone through that, I would not be who I am today."

CHAPTER SIX

ROAD SIDE ASSISTANCE:

HELP!

"Helping one person may not change the world, but it could impact the life they live forever."

There is a bad misconception that when you are the leader or in a position of leadership that you will always be ok. That is the farthest thing from the truth. Whether it be on the job, your business, your household/family, or in your group of friends, when you are a leader you are the light. As my pastor would say, you have the oil, or you are anointed. There is something special about you and people are drawn to you like a magnet. Everyone comes to you for everything like asking questions, borrowing money, telling you all of their business, or just asking for prayer and encouragement.

People just love to be around you. Whatever the case may be, you are the one they run to, and when they come, you pour into them. You speak life, you give them money, pray and intercede for people, mentor people, and you give new opportunities to people. It seems like you have literally been the one God chose to be the leader and to do this but let me ask you this question. After you have done all that, who's there to pour into you? I have seen a number of leaders, light carriers, and anointed people get discouraged and spiral downwards. I mean literally dropping the ball.

They used to be the one speaking life, and now they're not saying anything. They used to lend money and help people out; now you can't get them to give up a dollar. I mean true leaders who once had a vision and moved towards it with passion and purpose. Now they are sitting still, and it seems as if they can't even see the vision anymore. I'm asking what happened and the answers are all the same, "I'm tired, man." When you are the vehicle that God uses to be the light to His people, sometimes you can run out of gas. It's literally like driving on the open road, and you are stopping to help people on the way. One person here and another there, but never paying attention to your own gas tank. The next thing that happens is you find yourself stuck and unable to move because now your tank is on E (empty). Most people would say, "Gas up at a gas station," but instead of listening, you keep going.

One thing I found to be true is that leaders oftentimes neglect themselves. So, when it's time to gas up, they ignore it and say, "I'll do it later," never making the stop at the self-service to fill back up. They are not prepared when they hit a sudden unexpected stop. So now what do you do? Does the thought come to your mind to call Triple A? I use this analogy to illustrate the notion that when you're out of gas in your car, you call Triple A. Likewise when your gas is out in life, you call on God. Making it to your destiny is so important to God that He will send someone to fill you back up. He won't leave you on the side of the road. You have to be open to it because it may not come from who you expect. Oftentimes, we look for the people we helped to come help us, and because they don't, we become bitter and angry. Don't miss your blessing just because help doesn't come wrapped in the package you were expecting. God knows exactly what you need, and He may use a complete stranger to pour into you.

◉ HELP!!!

On this road we call life, I've had some really high moments, and I've had some low ones, but I can honestly say through it all, God has remained with me and never left me alone. I speak about being the light and running out of gas because I understand this condition all too well, because I live it and at some points, it's been my reality. For years, I have been the one that people come to. I've been the voice of reason to some and an encourager to others. Pouring love and inspiration into people every day, you would think I had it all together. I realized I was just as jacked up like the people I was trying to help. I have such a heart for people that their problems became my problems, their bills became my bills, and their pain became my pain. I was carrying the weight of my world and the worlds of the people I was pouring into. The heavier this load became, the more gas I had to burn just to move forward.

I started to notice my progress had slowed down; I wasn't moving as fast as I used to. I noticed not only passion slipping, but also my finances, and my mind was too. I was in a desperate place in my life at that moment, and as I looked around, I couldn't find anyone to help me. I was running to people, seeking their sympathy and for a listening ear, but instead, I got rejected. In some cases, the people that did listen, instead of helping me, ran and told my personal business to other people. Back and forth, back and forth, I was looking for people to help me and each time I came back empty. Then I realized I needed to stop looking around and start looking up. The Bible says in Psalms 121:1-2, "I will lift up my eyes to the hills, from whence comes my help. My help comes from the Lord." I stopped calling on people and started calling on the name of the Lord, and He answered.

I'll never forget while sitting in the car with my best friend, Kris. This night, in particular, I was at an all-time low. The stress of running my business had piled up on me, and mentally I was breaking down. Kris didn't mind me venting; he allowed me to let it all out. I couldn't believe where I was financially. I was literally broke, and my bills were piling up. I couldn't figure out how I was going to pay them. All the staff at the shop I either had to fire, or they left on their own.

So now I have no money and no staff. I was working every day just to play catch up and still couldn't get ahold of the bills. I was so disappointed in myself for ever letting things get this bad. To make matters worse, I couldn't figure out where I went wrong. Over and over again I kept asking myself, *What did I do wrong. Wasn't I a good leader? Was I fair? Did I overspend somewhere? What in the world happened?* I sat there in the passenger seat of my friend's car with tears in my eyes because I couldn't believe I was in this place. He looked at me and told me I was going to get through it. I felt a little comfort when he told me. God didn't bring me this far to leave me. He gave me some money, and we prayed.

Right after we finished praying, I got a phone call.

"Hello,"

"What's going on?" I said.

"Hi, my name is Lenny and I own a hair shop in the city, and one of my clients brought your name up."

I was sitting on the other side of the phone still confused as to why this guy was calling me, but I listened.

"My client and I were talking about luxury cars, and she made mention of you. She started talking about this young guy who would go sit at the dealership and take pictures with the car saying, one day he would have it."

I replied, "Yeah, that's me."

"I was so impressed by the story that I asked her to show me your page. I saw how you took it to the next level and taped the Bentley logo on your steering wheel."

"Yeah, I can't let myself forget my goals because I believe God will bless me with it one day if I keep believing."

We went on with this conversation for a while, talking about the luxury cars. For some reason, I was led to ask him about his business. He told me he had been in business for ten years at his current location. He had recently expanded the location by building a 1200 square foot addition to the back of it. There was no question this guy was successful and had some knowledge about being an entrepreneur. I asked how the ten years was and at first, he said what any businessman would say, it had been good.

I then started telling him about what was going on with me and my business. I wanted to be completely honest with the guy about everything, and I was surprised when he began to pour out. As I was talking he stopped me to interject, he said, "What you are going through is just part of the process. I have been through many ups and downs in my business, but they made me who I am today." He went on to share that he had been through some of the exact same things I was going through. He even admitted that he felt like he wanted to quit before, but he stuck it out, and it got better. Those were such simple words of encouragement that I needed at the time. He even spoke life into me as a person and told me he saw the blessings of the Lord on me, and that I was bigger than my current situation. He said I would go on and do great things and even said he saw me in that Bentley. We talked a little bit more and shared some concepts about life and business. He even referred me to a book for me to read to start my days off, *Commanding Your Morning* by Dr. Cindy Trimm. We closed the conversation and kept in contact afterward.

What amazed me was such a simple conversation from a complete stranger made the world of difference in my life. What I realized after that conversation was I had to get back to the grind and keep going to get past the situation. Businessman to businessman, he made me realize that what was happening wasn't uncommon and encouraged me that the best was yet to come. Struggles build character, and when it seems like you're going down, you are actually preparing to go up.

What I was experiencing is the roller coaster ride of life and entrepreneurship. I had been climbing steadily, then all of a sudden I began to take this nose dive down, and it looked like I was about to crash. It was not for me to be afraid, but rather sit back and enjoy the ride because that downward dive is building momentum for the upward movement that was coming into my life. Upward movement was exactly what happened after that conversation helped me put some things in perspective.

It was through continued prayer and planning that my execution was a short way away. Leaders, I understand the feeling of being alone. The feeling of wondering how I got to a place I never expected to be, and the feeling of how I am going to get out. Bring your petition to God and stop looking for people to come aid and assist you because your circle is not the answer. God will send someone to help you with whatever the case may be. He will provide you with what you need. Whether it's in your finances, an emotional or spiritual need, God will send someone to get you. Your name will be mentioned, and they'll be assigned to getting you back on the road. You will have to accept the help. If I had rejected the conversation that night, who knows where I would be now, but I didn't because I knew God was in it. I believe your help is just one call away.

CHAPTER SEVEN

TRAFFIC JAM:

Stay In Your LANE

"Good things come to those who wait."

It was in the month of March that I visited Los Angeles for the first time. This was a trip for leisure just to chill and relax with my girlfriend. Generally, at the beginning of the year, the first quarter is a busy time for me in my industry. I literally found myself working day in and out with no days off, so needless to say, a vacation was finally needed. I remember the excitement and anticipation I had as we walked through the terminal at Midway Airport in Chicago on our way to the West Coast. I had heard so much from my friends about all the different things to do in LA. Everything sounded exciting from shopping to the nightlife, and I couldn't wait to see what awaited us. Finally, the boarding process had started, I was walking quickly down the jet deck and on my way to finding our seats. We made it to our assigned seats and buckled up; then we were ready to take off. The plane started moving, and the excitement grew more and more as we began to ascend from the ground. Looking out the window, I remember saying, "LA here we come!"

After about four hours, we landed at LAX in Los Angeles. We

quickly darted through the airport to retrieve our bags and to pick up our car rental. After all the hustle and bustle, we finally secured our luggage and a vehicle. We headed to our hotel to get checked in. We entered the address into the GPS to our hotel in Beverly Hills. According to the route created by the GPS, it would take 45 minutes to reach our destination. So we buckled up and slapped in some music, then took off toward our LA adventure. Low and behold my excitement was short-lived, when I was introduced to an element of LA my friends didn't tell me about, and that was the traffic. The GPS put me on the 405 going north towards Beverly Hills, and I was immediately greeted by red brake lights and the sound of honking horns. Man, we were in a traffic jam like I've never experienced.

The cars were literally bumper to bumper and moving as slow as snails. After about ten minutes of inching forward and quickly hitting my brakes, I found myself looking to the left and to the right in search of a lane that was moving because mine was not. I saw movement in the far-left lane and worked my way over just to get there, and the lane stopped moving. Insane right? As I looked back over to my right, I noticed the lane I just left was proceeding ahead. I quickly put my turn signal back on and shot back into the lane I just left with hopes of making some advancement on this crowded freeway. The move was to no avail since the lane had stopped moving. I must have looked like a madman on that freeway; my head was moving left to right like a metronome looking for a fast lane to move forward and get to our destination. In the midst of all my frustration, I was still able to hear my girlfriend say something to me that was so profound I'll never forget it, she said, "Baby, stay in your lane."

♥ STAY IN YOUR LANE

We live in a society where more people are leaving the

traditional nine to five job or skipping college, and they are jumping into the world of entrepreneurship. New ideas and businesses are being born every day, but not many of them are able to last very long. The question is, why? The concept or idea of becoming an entrepreneur today is promoted widely, and it is constantly encouraged. I mean just the title itself holds so much weight. It's sexy, it flows so eloquently, and it demands a certain level of regard for the name that it's attached to. I can hear some of the people now. "Hello. My name is Blank, and I'm an entrepreneur." But what I've come to find is that most people want the title more then they want the job.

They want profits more then they want the process. They want to see the fruit from the business they planted, but they are not willing to wait for the seed to spread its roots. Where there are no roots, there can be no fruit. So when the business is not doing what they thought it would do or is not growing fast enough, they put it down, and guess what? They are just like me in that traffic jam. Their excitement fades, and they find themselves looking around for more opportunities, jumping from lane to lane, business to business, idea to idea, never really mastering anything. Just owning things, they are not willing to take care of just to say they own it. Obviously, they did not realize that if you're going to have ownership, you need to have stewardship. Switching lanes, a new job today, new venture tomorrow—STOP! And just stay in your lane.

What do I mean by staying in your lane? The expression simply is a metaphor for just basically being still. When you stay in your lane, you stay in a place long enough to master it. You get rooted in it and grounded in it, and you build a strong foundation. In this ever-growing society, it seems as if the concept of being grounded or building foundations is a thing of the past. People want everything quickly. This is the time of social media where you can reach thousands in seconds or go viral and become a star overnight. So taking the slow route and building is not ideal to most people but let me tell you this: In order for your gift, talent, or business to flourish the way it needs to flourish, you'll need to be grounded. If you are not, you'll find out that your gifts and talents will take you places your character can't keep you. They'll take you places you have not been groomed for, places you have not been prepared for, and places you haven't been built to handle. Ask yourself, if God really gave you the success you are looking for, would you be ready?

There is a blessing in laying a strong foundation and being grounded. The Bible tells us in Matthew 7:24-25 about a house that was built on a rock. It says wise men build their house on a rock. The rain will come down, the streams will rise, and the winds will blow and beat against that house, but it will not fall because it has a foundation that was built on a rock. The benefit of foundation-building is that when the trials of life come, you'll be able to handle it—and they will come. Remember this, storms come to test your foundation, and its purpose is to see if you are grounded or not. The purpose is not to take you out, so don't panic. People will look to you to be grounded. They'll look to see your stability, and they will look to you to be steadfast and unmovable. In business and in life, there is no real way to plan for disruption because it comes so unexpectedly. But if you build on a strong rock that is a good foundation, you won't fall, and the people that are following you won't bail out.

⚲ POURING THE CONCRETE

Now some of you may be saying, ok, we understand that foundations are important, but how do you begin to build one? The answer to that question is pretty simple my friends, and it's to study. The first priority of a new entrepreneur is to investigate the industry that you wish to be in. Learning it in and out, and from front to back, researching to find out the successes and the failures of other similar businesses and learn from them. It's vital that you do not miss this part of the process. I believe it's one of the most important because studying is the preliminary stage before you plan to lay your foundation. With that information, you want to take it and do what I call a SWOT analysis. SWOT is an acronym that stands for strengths, weaknesses, opportunities, and threats. You want to analyze your strengths, weaknesses, opportunities, and threats in whatever industry you choose to do business. This will help you build and develop a strategy moving forward and create some cognitive solutions to deploy when you start your business.

After you have studied, it's now time to start planning. Planning is writing your dream out. The Bible says in Habakkuk 2:2 to write the vision and make it plain so that they who read it will run. That means if you write it out people will work to build it. This is your blueprint stage of building a strong foundation, and without a blueprint, builders can't build. This is where you'll answer questions like: What does this business look like? How does it operate? and How will it be marketed? For example, a year and a half before I opened my first business, I called up my boys who were doing what I was doing as far as our industry goes. I dropped the concept of all of us coming together and working under one roof. We all had different qualities, and there was a lot of diversity, but I believed if we brought all that together it would create a great synergy, and we would be as strong as a force of nature.

We all came together and met at my mother's house. At the time, I was living with her, and I was working out of the back bedroom. Never allow yourself to be discouraged because of your small beginnings. Keep in mind that big things come from humble beginnings. Apple was started in a garage, Facebook was started in a college dorm room, and your vision or dream will start right where you are if you dare to believe. Never forget that. So we all met there and sat down at the kitchen table. We started by writing out a plan for this business. I was sitting at one end of the table looking at three other guys, and we had one on the phone to chime in. Interestingly, none of us had experience in opening this kind of business, but what we did have was the audacious attitude that we were going to get this done. We sat there with faith and developed a plan for what was to happen for years to come. I recommend you do the same thing, start planning.

The next step in this process I call framing. After you have written the vision, you now have to go find someone who has done what you are trying to do and allow them to teach you through mentorship. I believe in leadership follower-ship. In order to be a good leader, you have to be a great follower. It tells us this in Psalm 37:37, "Mark the perfect man." There are great benefits in mentorship, and if you are blessed to connect with the right one, it will change the whole trajectory of your life." I'll never forget the first time I met one of my mentors, Malachi Gary; it's a funny story. I walked into this guy's shop. I was young, motivated, and ambitious looking for a job. I was so arrogant, and I just knew he would hire me because my presentation was impeccable. I set up my laptop and start scrolling through the pictures, thoroughly convinced I had the job. Well, he didn't hire me. Instead, he told me I needed more development; he said get more practice and come back after a year, and we could revisit the conversation. Those were his words verbatim, and he said it so sternly I couldn't do anything but say ok and walk out the door. I didn't know then, neither did he, but the next time we would meet our conversation would be different.

So fast forward three years later. My business had accelerated to a high level, and I was producing some of the best quality work you could find in my city. I had a growing and revolving clientele, and I was working every day, so it's safe to say I was doing alright. Malachi had made some advancements as well. When we first met, he had that one tattoo shop. Since that time, he had opened two more that were successful. So it was safe to say he wasn't doing so bad for himself either. Around this time, I decided I wanted to open the business, and who else better to show me how then the man who now owned three? I called him up and arranged a meeting. The most amazing part about this is how God will place people in your life at the appointed time. When I first met him, I was looking to get a job, but God placed him in my life to teach me how to give jobs. It didn't work out how I wanted it in the beginning because it wasn't in God's plan. Now things were falling in line because the timing was right.

Let this be a lesson; it's all in the timing. We met, and I shared with him what I was planning to do, and without hesitation, he grabbed my hand and walked me through the process. Within a year's time that I was with him, I learned everything I needed to know, from the structure to managing staff, creating accounts with vendors, getting licensed. I was blessed that he taught me everything. He got me ready, and to this day, I run my ideas by him, and he advises me in life and in business. Mentorship is so important because you can't become something you've never seen. Mark the perfect man and find someone to show you how to get where you want to go.

After you have done all this, you are now ready. It's time to pour. Pouring the concrete is the last stage of building your foundation; it's the execution stage. This is where you take everything you've learned, everything you've studied, and everything you've planned and begin to build your vision from the ground up. This will require some hard work and patience, but good things come to those who are willing to wait. Oh yeah, and before I forget, let me tell you what ended up happening with my girlfriend and me in this LA traffic jam. Because I decided to stay in my lane, I was able to see what was happening ahead. The traffic was moving slowly, and I noticed there was some construction going on, so I looked down at the GPS and found a route that would take us around the traffic. We quickly put our plan into action and took the next exit to the right. Because we chose to take this route, we ended up saving time and arrived at our hotel with five minutes to spare. When you stay in your lane, it allows you to see what's going on ahead and plan for it. Apply the same concept to building your vision. Stop, study, and plan; you are closer than you think.

● STOPPED RIGHT IN THE MIDDLE

You didn't think I forgot about you, did you? Yes, you, the one reading this right now. I can hear you saying to yourself right now that this was a nice chapter, with some really helpful tips, but I'm not trying to open a business. Entrepreneurship is not for me, I have a good job, and I'm cool. You already have a foundation in life, and it is set in stone. As far as you are concerned, you're good. But—I can almost bet you are wondering why you can't seem to go higher? I mean we all do. It's almost like you have hit a glass ceiling in your life, and everything you have tried to do to advance is not working. Whether it's on the job, in your relationship, or simply in life, nothing is working, and it's almost like you're stuck. You are in a traffic jam. Does this sound familiar? If so, this is a special part I am writing just for you. Check this out, I want to tell you a story.

Allow me to take you back, let's say about ten years. My work hadn't taken off for me yet if I remember correctly. I don't believe I'd even started tattooing yet. I think I was in between stages of looking for a job and trying to go to school. Basically, I was broke and hustling—an odd job here and there, just doing what I could to make some money. I ended up landing a little job with my mother's landlord, helping him rehab a new home he had just acquired. I wasn't doing much; I wasn't the carpenter, the plumber, not even the electrician. I was the labor boy, and my job was to go in, tear everything out, and put it in the dumpster outside. I'm talking old cabinets, sinks, old soggy carpets—you know all that good stuff. I was carrying this old rubbish out on my back, hauling it into the dumpster for ten hours a day. Sounds like fun, right? Yeah, I know. I had a lot of it. Seriously, don't despise hard work. It builds character, at least that's what they told me. Back to the story. I finally get the house cleaned out, and the real guys came in and started to do their work. What was once an ugly empty shell had begun to turn into this beautiful masterpiece in only about two weeks' time. I mean these guys had done an awesome job.

This place had new windows, a new roof, a beautiful interior with an open concept, all new appliances—this house was the bomb, and it wasn't even finished yet. But one day all of a sudden we just had to stop. I know you're probably asking, why? I certainly needed to know because this job is how I was getting paid. Well, this is why: the plumber on the project was in the basement working on some pipes and noticed some huge cracks in the foundation. The foreman overseeing the project told us to stop because the weight of the house could not be supported by this cracked foundation. I know you are probably reading this and wondering what in the world am I talking about, which leads me to ask you this next question: Are there any cracks in your foundation that you are aware of? You see, we get stuck in life and find ourselves unable to move forward. I believe we get too comfortable or for lack of a better word, I'm going to say, negligent. Neglecting to address the small issues that we know about ourselves, we forget to do a self-check. We forget our core values and focus more on our advantages in life. We want more of the job, the money, and the success at the expense of our purpose. A lot of people become frustrated because they are not moving forward. There are those who look for their degrees and talents to advance them. The world promotes you based on your talents, but God promotes you based on your heart. I believe God has you here because He is saying stop, it's time for me to check your foundation.

● FILLING THE CRACKS

Let's talk. When you fill the cracks, you get balanced. A house that sits on a cracked foundation becomes off balanced because of its weight. This imbalance will cause the foundation to shift, and the house will be unstable. In life, when we are all negligent in some areas and if we ignore the cracks in our foundation, we can also become unstable just like that house. On the outside, we'll look good, but underneath the surface, we are all beat up. What are the cracks? Cracks are those character flaws that we all have because no one is perfect. They consist of the things we hide and cover up so no one can see. These are things we pick up in life. They could stem from childhood, past relationships, circumstances, or the environment. It can be our own personal baggage that we hold on to. I will just name a few: hurt, pain, insecurities, anger, jealousy, and envy. We are all different, but we all have flaws. For some, it may be depression. It has a hold on you secretly, and on the outside, you are all smiles, but on the inside, you are dying. Yes, it's possible to be blessed and depressed. For others, it can be your attitude. One minute you can be fine, but the minute someone says the wrong thing you pop off and curse them out.

There are so many people who are anointed, talented, and gifted, but they are meaner than the devil himself. Wondering why you can't go higher, it's because of the foundation. The heart isn't right. God wants to take you higher, but your heart has to be right. It says in Proverbs 4:23, "Above all else, guard your heart because everything you do flows from it." It's impossible to go higher and be impactful if your heart isn't right. You will be unbalanced, and everything you do will reflect it. Guarding your heart means fixing it and addressing the things you know that are not right. How do we fix it? We bring it to God. The Bible tells us to give all your burdens to the Lord, and He will take care of you. You have to literally bring that thing in front of God. The time I'm working on it or trying to get over it is done, and the time is now. If you will make the choice, God will make the change.

I began to pray and ask God to create in me a clean heart and renew in me the right spirit. God said in His word; I will overturn, overturn, overturn it, and it shall be no more. So while you are praying, God is turning things over. He's turning over depression, turning over past hurt and pain, turning over thoughts of suicide. He's beginning to work on the cracks in your foundation. He is breaking you down to build you back up.

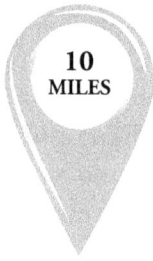

CHAPTER EIGHT

FLAT TIRE:

You Can FIX IT

"There is more inside of you dig deep, and you will find."

I'll always remember my first experience wrestling with a flat tire. Man, was it a headache. I was driving from Chicago to Atlanta to visit my little sister for her 21st birthday. She had moved there a year prior, and we hadn't seen each other since she left. She was feeling homesick but couldn't come back to Chicago because of her work schedule. I saw this as a great opportunity to go there and surprise her so we could reconnect, catch up, and we could celebrate her birthday together. I packed my bags, put gas in the car, and headed off to Atlanta. It was about twelve noon when I left, and the GPS said it was roughly a ten-hour trip. I've driven to Atlanta on a number of occasions so I could get there in about eight hours. Now I'm not going to say I was speeding. Let's just say I was driving a lot faster than the other cars on the road. Moving with a purpose from highway to highway, through city to city, side road to side road, lost by the sound of my music. I didn't realize I was six hours into my trip and I was making good time.

All of a sudden, it began to rain. It started off slowly as a light drizzle, softly laying on the windshield almost like a blanket of dew on the morning grass. Then it began to hit a little bit harder. I don't know if it was just me, but it seemed as if the farther I went down the highway, the harder the rain began to fall. A bright bolt of lightning shot across the night sky followed by the sound of traffic humming from the adjacent road. BOOM—a loud crash of thunder sounded off, startling me and causing the hairs to rise on the back of my neck. Then the rain came, rushing down, hitting the windshield like a tsunami. If I was to tell you that I was terrified, it would be an understatement. My heart was beating out of my chest because I couldn't see a thing. It was like my windshield wipers weren't moving fast enough. So I began to slow the car down and started to drift over to the shoulder of the road. Somewhere in between me changing lanes, I hit a pothole and didn't realize my back-right tire popped. I heard the sound but didn't think anything of it until the rear end of the car started to shake. "You gotta be kidding me," I remember saying to myself as I pulled onto the shoulder of the road.

⦿ THE STORM

I don't know what it is about this journey we call life, but it's almost like when things are already going bad, somehow they find a way to get worse. It never seems to fail. Sometimes all you can do is just shake your head. I mean for real, let's be honest. We all have had some situations in life where life itself has knocked us down, and in the middle of getting back up, something else happens to bring us back to our knees. For instance, you could be living paycheck to paycheck, struggling to provide and pay your bills, then all of a sudden you'll lose your job. How many of us have been there? What am I going to do? and then you ask yourself, "What's next? As you sit in a pool of anxiety and fear, pray, pray, and pray some more is what people are telling you, but it seems like God is not answering you. What do you do when life keeps swinging?

You fight back. The Bible says in Romans 8:18, "That the suffering of this present time is not worthy to be compared with the glory which shall be revealed in us." God is saying, I put something in you, and the purpose of this storm is to bring it out.

God has prepared you for such a time as this. For example, let me tell you about a particular woman in the Bible. She is mentioned in 2 Kings 4:1-7. We don't know her name, but we know she had a problem, and it was getting worse. Her problem was that she was a widow; her husband had died. We have all lost someone in life, and the process of grieving is no joke. We can only imagine the struggle she was facing. The Bible also tells us she had two sons. So not only was she a widow and had lost the love of her life, but she has now become a single mother that had to raise two boys on her own. I can almost see that woman sitting in a room, looking at those boys and her situation, rocking back and forth, crying and wondering what was she going to do next. Her husband, her lover, the provider and protector of that house, was no longer there. Now she had to find a way to cope with being alone and raising their two boys to be men. In She was going through, and in the midst of her disparity, while she was faced with this type of anxiety and unrest, life found a way to hit her again. Her husband's creditors were coming to collect a debt. She didn't have the money to pay them, and now they wanted to take her sons.

The situation went from bad to worse, and now she was at risk of losing her children. In a state of panic and as a cry for help, she ran to the prophet Elisha, the man her husband had walked with before his demise. She told him all about her issues. He listened to her distress and then asked her a question. "What do you have in your house?" At first, the woman told him nothing, then she thought about it a bit longer and said, "A small jar of olive oil." The prophet then told her to go to her neighbors and ask for empty jars. He put emphasis for her not to just ask for a few jars but as many as she could. He went on to tell her that after doing this, to go home and begin to pour the olive oil into the jars, and so she did. I could only imagine how her living room must have looked. It was probably a mess with jars everywhere. Jar after jar she began pouring, working together with her sons as she filled the jars. She poured until there was not another jar left, and then the oil stopped flowing. She went back and told Elisha. The prophet instructed her to sell the jars to pay off the debts, and she and her sons could live off the rest. There was enough money left over to provide for her and the two sons.

This is an excellent example of faith and using what God has already provided. No matter the size or significance, God can take what is not enough and make it more than enough. This amazing woman, I call her amazing because of the faith she displayed in the midst of this storm, was hit by a life-altering experience. There was no way for her to know that her provision would come in the form of a small jar sitting on her shelf. That little jar of olive oil that didn't look like it would be enough turned out to provide her with more than she needed. She got a word from the Lord and used what He already set in place. I want to ask you this, "What do you have?"

♦ EVERYTHING YOU NEED IS RIGHT THERE

As I was sitting on the side of this road, I knew I couldn't sit there for very long. I had to figure something out. I looked at my phone and tried to dial roadside assistance, but because of the storm, I couldn't seem to get a signal through. So I figured if I was going to get off the side of this road, I was going to have to change the tire myself. So I grabbed a hoodie that I had in the back seat and put it on in an effort to block the rain and get out of the car. The wind was blowing so hard I was pushed against the side of the car as I exited the vehicle. Oh, and the rain—it was coming down so fast and hard that I was soaked within minutes. It turns out that the hoodie really didn't make much difference. Fighting through this wind and rain, I finally made it to the back of the car to access the trunk. I opened it and was quickly reminded how unorganized I was. I say it humorously, but I mean it. My trunk was a mess. It was full of stuff, and there was junk everywhere. As I was sifting through all this mess, I remembered my older brother showing me how to change a tire. I knew I would need a tire iron, a jack or a lift, and of course the spare tire. To my amazement after scrambling through all this junk, I found all the pieces. So I pulled them all out one at a time and set them on the ground. I stepped back and looked at everything and remembered what to do. I got down on one knee, jacked that car up and went to work. What is so profound about this experience was this: Everything that I needed was already in the car; it was built with it.

It is important that you understand as you are going through this time in life, this unexpected hardship, this storm with the flat tire, that God has built you with all the tools. He knew before you were even born what you would need to get back moving and back on this road we call life. This is not the end for you. You have to ask yourself what else do I have inside, what other seeds has God planted in you. What is that one thing in your life that you've always wanted to do, but you didn't give it much attention? You could love to work out and go to the gym; you could take that skill and desire and become a trainer. You could have the talent to sing, and maybe you've been singing all your life and never paid attention that you could become a successful recording artist. I have been drawing pictures on paper my entire life, as early as I can remember. One day I decided to use that talent, and now I am a business owner. So understand that God has equipped you with more than one gift. It's up to you to explore what those gifts are, and if you have faith, He will bless them. What was once little, He will make big. Sift through the mess and the junk of life and find your divine gifts and tools that will move you forward. Also, notice that when I tried to call roadside assistance, I couldn't get through. I hate to be the bearer of bad news, but no one is coming to get you. It's not going to just fall out the sky either; you have to do the work.

There are so many people today that just sit and wait on God to move in situations like these. I'm not saying you shouldn't pray, because you should, but you have to be both spiritual and practical; you will have to get your hands dirty. The Bible says, "Faith without works is dead," so understand you must pray with one hand and work with the other. You could be waiting on God, and God could very well be waiting for you to make a move. I had to get out of the car, out of the comfort and safety of the driver seat, onto a busy highway, where cars were flying past me at upward speeds of 80 mph. Needless to say, I was terrified in my soul in the midst of a thunderstorm when I had to change that flat tire.

The widow woman in the Bible lost her husband and was left to raise two sons on her own. Emotionally she was broken and gripped by the fear of losing her sons, and that's what forced her to get up and make a move. What am I saying? You have to get outside your comfort zone and face this current storm head-on. I'm saying it's in the scariest moments of life when you have to make a move and through the toughest time when you have to believe. Get up! Every successful person I know or have read about had a scary place where they didn't think they would make it out. There is one thing they all had in common, and that was they made a move. You can either sit there and wait for nothing to happen or make a move and see the hand of God move in your situation. So my question to you is what are you waiting to do? What is it? Where is it? What do you have? And don't let your age hold you back either. I hear so many people today say "I'm too old," baby Bye. God can still use you, and there is still something inside of you.

You are only limited in life by your own creativity. Take a look at the woman and the olive oil again; we can suspect by the scripture that she is not a young woman, so her age was not a factor. Now, where is the seed God planted? Some would look at the jar of olive oil. She followed the prophet's instruction and poured the oil, and it didn't stop until she ran out of jars because God blessed it. I like to believe God also placed an entrepreneurial seed inside of her. It was her faith and the actions she took in the midst of her struggles that enabled her to get what she needed and wake up what was already there. She was faced with a series of heart-wrenching experiences. First, she lost her husband, now his creditors were after her and last but not least, she faced losing her sons. These circumstances led her to the olive oil, along with her sons they worked pouring the oil, and then she sold the oil, and it got here out of debt. I may not be the smartest man in the world, but that sounds like she started a business to me. The struggles, the storm, were all necessary and they had to happen. The olive oil was just the tool God used to provide what she needed in that season of her life. It's often in the place of your greatest frustration, your scary place, that God will reveal His greatest glory.

♥ THERE IS LIGHT AT THE END

It seems so cliché to say it will get better later, but no matter how much you may not want to believe it, life has demonstrated that it always stand to be true. It really will! After I went through this mess, fighting the storm and this flat tire that popped up out of nowhere, I was eventually able to get back on the road. Let me tell you, it felt so good to get off the side of that highway. As I began to drive, I was about two miles back into my trip, and the rain had started to slow down. The vicious tsunami had simmered down to a lite sprinkle. The dark clouds split like the Red Sea, exposing the beautiful night sky. There sat the moon, perfectly in place, accompanied by a great multitude of stars, all resting in the hands of God. It was beautiful. I rolled down my window, and a fresh gust of wind floated through the muggy car, reintroducing the aroma of a cool summer night. I was able to take a deep breath finally. As I digress, I once heard a speaker say, "Pain is temporary. It may last for a second, an hour, or even a day, but eventually, it will subside, and something else will take its place." You must understand that after you have made your move and you have done the work, your current storm will pass. Something else will take its place, and I believe that is peace. The Bible says, "Better is the end of a thing than the beginning." Just know that you are coming out of this better than you went in.

10 MILES

CHAPTER NINE

CRUISING:

Enjoy The RIDE

"Self-preservation is the first law of nature."

Panting and struggling to catch my breath, the world around me was spinning. What was happening to me? I was battling to move my limbs, like my hands. *If I could just bend my fingers,* I remember thinking. As I tried, nothing was happening. Instead, my mobility was replaced by a tingling sensation that traveled from my fingertips all the way up my arm. *It's hot out here,* I said to myself, *I need some water.* Then all of a sudden came the heart palpitations. Out of nowhere, my chest was beating like a college drum line on homecoming night. I really felt like I needed to sit down. I started looking around for somewhere to sit, and that's when I noticed a bus stop. I scurried my way towards it, and my vision started to get blurry. Blinking my eyes, I was trying to regain my focus. With every second that passed, I tried opening and closing my eyes, but the bus stop bench suddenly seemed further and further away. *If you could just get there,* the voice in my head was saying. Wait, something was happening. My body was starting to shake. Out of fear and desperation, I tried to take a step forward, and down I went. Falling to the ground, my stiff body slammed against the hard pavement just inches

76

away from the bus stop. "Help! Help! Somebody help me," I tried to yell, but I couldn't seem to utter a word.

Staring into the sky as the hot summer sun beamed off the beads of sweat on my forehead, I couldn't help but feel helpless. *What's happening to me?* "Help!" I called out one more time in hopes that someone would hear me. A young man walking past heard the whisper-like cry. He turned his head towards me, looked down and said, "Are you alright?" He saw that my body was shaking, and he grabbed my cold and clammy hands and said, "I'm going to get some help." There I was, lying on the ground, my body paralyzed, and my mind slipping in and out of consciousness. The only thing I could hear was the muffled sound of this young man's voice saying, "Somebody call 911," then everything went black. I had no idea that on July 19, 2011, my life would be turned upside down.

The human body is an amazing work of art. It has a funny way of talking and letting you know there's something wrong with it and when you don't listen, it screams. This was a scream. My body was saying, "HEY! SLOW DOWN!" Up until that day, I thought of myself as a pretty healthy guy. I wasn't out of shape; I think I had a pretty decent diet—ramen noodles and fried chicken, you know stuff like that. I'm talking average 20-year-old stuff, but I soon realized I was all wrong. I'm going to take you back three days prior. I had a rush of clients at the tattoo shop, so I was working literally 48 hours straight. Yeah, I was getting that money. I took some small breaks in between, but my main focus was getting paid. So I did just that, I got paid. I had so much going on at the time, and I was saving to open a new location, and also saving to buy a new car. I had my regular bills, and on top of that, I was paying for a billboard on the highway. My daily grind was turned all the way up.

Working like this was not unusual for me. It was my culture, and I was used to being in the shop all night, but back to my story. I tattooed all these clients, got paid, and finally headed home. I couldn't wait to get in the bed, but when I got there I was met with some bad news—someone had stolen my dog. Now I know some of you might be reading this and thinking, this guy can't be serious. Well, guess what? I am, and it's not funny. Actually, I was devastated when I found this out. Stress literally kicked me in my back, and I was losing my mind. "KJ!" I yelled out as I walked the streets. For hours I was out there looking, but I couldn't find him anywhere. While this was going on, my phone was ringing off the hook. It was one of my friends who was having a birthday party, and I was supposed to be there hosting. I was stressed out about my dog, tired from work, and still hadn't gotten any sleep. Despite my better judgment, I answered my phone and said, "I'm on my way." What in the world was I thinking? I hosted the party, and it turned out to be a long night, to say the least. It was now morning, and again I was headed home to get some sleep. At this point, all I wanted to do was lie down. I was running my body like crazy and stressing my mind to the limit with frivolous things that didn't matter. I never expected on that beautiful summer day at that bus stop, I would fall out and have two Grand mal seizures.

♀ UNPLUG

Let's have some real conversation here. How many of you can honestly say, "I work too much"? It's ok to raise your hands. I'm not there, but I can feel you. Also, how many of you can say, "I'm too hard on myself"? You too? I thought it was just me. Cool, let's talk. In this ever-growing society, there are so many things to keep the inquisitive mind intrigued—things that inspire, things that motivate, things that will drive you to new heights. No matter what level you are on in life, just being alive can inspire you to think bigger, work harder, and do better, as it should. It can birth an audacious attitude in you that believes you can reach all of your goals. It can give you such a tenacious drive that you'll go after those goals relentlessly. Nonstop day in and day out, working to reach those goals, but let me ask you this.: "At what cost?" What do your relationships look like? Is your household in order? Is your spouse happy? How is your health? Oh, and the million-dollar question is: Are you happy? These are questions that today's workaholics struggle to avoid facing.

We run from answering those questions by doing more work. More often than not when those questions do come across our mind, we try to force them to the back of our mind. Reason being, we don't want to think about them. Who wants to face the embarrassment of realizing that the answer to most of them is no. In all honesty, you'd probably have to admit that you're not happy. Why aren't you happy? You would think that because one's work ethic is very strong, life would be amazing for them. I mean it's no secret that successful people who work hard have money and a lot of stuff—the big house, the nice car, and the fat bank account. How are you and the people around you not happy? You see, with money you can buy stuff, but you can't buy happiness. But it's happiness that you feel you need at that moment. I remember the time when I was a teenager, and I used to spend time on the block with the old heads. Old heads are the older men in the neighborhood who had some form of success. They bought tangible things, and most of it came from their illegal activity, but they were also street smart. So I would sit with these guys and pick up on some of the knowledge they would drop in their conversations.

One day when I was sitting out there, this guy looked at me and pulled out a large bankroll of money. He said, "You see this, lil dude. Either you're going to be a guy with time, or you're going to be a guy with money. Understand a guy with money ain't got no time, and a guy with time ain't got no money, which one will you be?" He then told me to get out of their conversation and go get some money. It was that conversation, that age-old riddle was something I lived by until I got older and found myself in the hospital. I was suffering from stress, sleep deprivation, malnourishment, and dehydration. I lay there, shaking my head, thinking to myself, *This dude lied to me.* That wisdom he dropped on me had to be wrong because if this was the result, heck I'd rather be broke and have my time. I strongly believed I could have both time and money. So that day, I challenged the age-old riddle and found my answer. It was through creating a work-life balance.

If you've never heard the term "work-life balance," you're probably wondering what it is. Well, a work-life balance is just that, balance. It's when you take your professional and your personal life, and you go through the strenuous process of balancing the two. I say strenuous because it is not easy. I remember when I first tried this. I said, "You know what, I got some money saved, so I'll just chill on work for a while." I found out it was easy to balance work and life when there was no work—until I started to go broke. Then I had to go back to the drawing board. As you can see, cutting off your job isn't the best answer, even though most of us would love for it to be. So I decided to come up with a schedule and try to live my life by it. It would be a fully detailed agenda for my day that would ensure I made time for me and maintained balance.

This is how I laid it out: I would get up in the morning from a full night's rest, eat a good nutritious breakfast, call my girlfriend to tell her good morning and that I love her. Then I would put on my workout clothes and hit the gym for an hour and come home to shower. I'd get dressed, eat a snack, and then call my mother. Next, I would head to work and tattoo for three hours, then go to lunch with my guys. Afterward, I'd go back to work and tattoo for another three hours, then head home. I would get home and play a little Call of Duty on the PlayStation, eat dinner, read a little, and go to bed. It was foolproof, but let me ask you this, how many days do you think I can actually live like that? You are absolutely right, not many. I soon realized a schedule like that was not going to work. I had to be realistic about the balance I was trying to create in my life. It didn't take long for me to come to an understanding that it wasn't going to come by making myself a slave to this ridiculous schedule. You wouldn't believe how many Americans live their lives like this in search of a healthy work-life balance. Without even realizing it, they become slaves to scheduling and micromanaging their lives day to day. It's obvious that scheduling is not the answer. What could it be? This was a journey I embarked on for the next couple of years, trying to get it right, searching to find the right balance to serve myself and the relationships around me.

One day my little brothers were at my shop on a Friday night. I was just finishing up a tattoo, and I was in the process of closing the shop. As I was turning off the lights and getting ready to lock the door, one of my brothers, the youngest out of the two, asked me if they could spend the night at my house. It had not dawned on me until then, but I realized I hadn't spent much time with my little brothers. Most of the time, they only saw me when I was working at the shop. I told him, yes, and we all loaded up in my car and headed to my house. When we finally arrived, I set them up on the game system and made us dinner. We played some NBA 2k and a little Call of Duty on the PlayStation, ate dinner, and talked until we fell asleep on my couch. The next morning after we got up, I made breakfast. I took them to the local museum, and we look around for a couple of hours. They were so amazed by some of the exhibits the museum had on display, and we talked about how much they were learning. When we were leaving, I came up with the idea to feed their ambition and plant a seed of desire into their young minds. They were quite surprised when I took them to the Bentley Gold Coast in Downtown Chicago. Once they got inside, they were all excited as they looked at all the beautiful cars. We even had the opportunity to sit in the driver seat of Lamborghinis, Bentleys, Aston Martins, a Rolls Royce, and a number of other exotic cars. That day I told them they could have any one of those cars. They just had to believe in it. It was so funny to see them arguing back and forth with each other as we left, saying, "That's my car. No, that's my car." It was truly a delight. I dropped them back off at my mother's house. I could tell when they got out of the car, they were full of joy. Before going into the house, they told me that was the best time they ever had. I thought about that; I didn't buy them a new game system. We didn't go to any sporting events. They were just happy to chill out with their older brother.

As I watched them go to the front door something clicked, and it all made sense. It's the small things in life that matter, the little things. These are the moments that constitute true happiness, and that makes it all worth it. Taking the time out to be there when it matters is, in my opinion, how you create a work-life balance. In the professional world, people are always going to be pulling on you from the left and from the right, but you have to decipher who gets priority. People are going to be disappointed. You just have to make sure it's not the same person every time. All it takes is small investments of your time in the right areas, and you can radically transform the quality of your relationships and the quality of your life. If more people started to do this, we could begin to change societies definition of success from the moronic notion that the man who dies with the most money wins to a more thoughtful and balanced definition of what a life well-lived looks like.

⦿ LIVE YOUR BEST LIFE

There is nothing like driving on the open road and slapping the car into cruise control. You can sit back and just enjoy the ride. Sometimes, we have to put our lives in cruise control and enjoy the ride on this road we call life. Oftentimes, we forget even though we are moving and working towards something in life to enjoy the process. We need to celebrate life and our own individual accomplishments. You wouldn't believe how many people today are like robots. They go to work, then come home just to do it all over again. They look up and every day, month after month, year after year, they're feeding the same time clock, trading time for a dollar and getting ripped off every time. Social life is disappearing outside of work, and little clicks are being built on the job. Long story short, you find yourself lonely and unhappy. The Bible says you will enjoy the fruits of your labor. Some of you may say that you do, but the truth is there are probably more people working jobs they hate to buy things to impress people they don't like. That's not enjoying the fruits of your labor. You have to get out there and enjoy this life. You'll have to get past the point of "I'll have a life when I retire" and start living now.

Take some time off to travel and go on a vacation. Statistics reports that only 35% of Americans took a vacation this year. I'd say that percentage means more than half of us kept our butts at home, probably bored and angry at having to work in the morning. This cannot be living. The Bible even says we need peace and a vacation every now and again. If you don't believe me, believe this. I love the Bible because it states in Psalm 23:2, "He makes me lie down in green pastures, he leads me beside still waters, and he restores my soul." By now you can tell I have a creative mind, so when I read, "He leads me beside still waters," my mind instantly thought of a beach in Aruba. I heard the waters are real still over there. No seriously though, what the green pastures and the still waters represent is peace. God wants to lead you to a place of peace in your life so He can restore you. The stresses of life can become heavy, and through vacationing, you can live a little and drop that stress. Also, you attend to the things that keep you balanced. For example, your intellect, your emotions, and your spirituality—these are all the areas God can pour back into you when you take time for you. So if you haven't already started planning your next trip, get your passport together because God is going to show you green pastures and still waters all over the world. Get ready and take time for you. Don't wait and find yourself saying, "I should've, could've, or would've," years down the line. Live your best life today and truly enjoy the fruits of your labor, spoil yourself sometimes and celebrate you. That's an idea worth sharing. Say to yourself today, "I will live my best life." Now live.

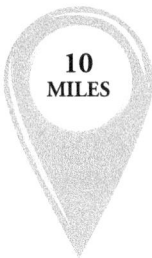

CHAPTER TEN

ARRIVED:

Reach BACK

"Do more for the world than the world does for you, that is success."

"In five hundred feet, turn left, and your destination will be on the right. Arrived."

Those words are like heaven when you have been on a long journey traveling somewhere. From hitting potholes to fixing flat tires, and even running out of gas— these may happen on your trip trying to make it to your destination. We live in a world full of problems you never expected when you started the trip, but despite all the adversity, you got there. So to hear that word "arrived" will have you leaping for joy because now you can take a deep breath. In life, we share that same feeling when we finally make it and live out our dreams. Whatever goal you started with, if it was to start a business, build a ministry, or maybe something personal like improving yourself, it was God who gave it to you. Now that you finally can touch it and everything has come to pass, my God, that's a feeling that words can't explain. You have finally made it, but the question is: What's next? I've got news for you; the work doesn't stop here. There is more to do. Making it to your destiny is not the end all be all. You are not finished, you are actually just getting started. Remember at the beginning of the book I said to you, "Destiny is God's destination for your life." His purpose is the reason that you are even on the road. I said that to inform you that destiny is never-ending—it doesn't stop. The Bible tells us that we go from glory to glory.

There is another level you're about to tap into now that you have made it to your destination/destiny, and that's "purpose." Ask yourself, why did God choose me to carry out this dream? I believe the reason God blesses His people and allows us to be successful is that He wants us to give back. His purpose is that He wants to use your success to be a blessing to the world. You will be given opportunities to be an answer to someone's prayer and to help them. Ephesians 2:10 states, "For we are his workmanship, created in Christ Jesus for good works." We are the vessels God will use. You didn't make it this far for no reason. It is time to give back. This is a concept that some successful people miss, the giving back part.

The culture today is a selfish culture. Everything is about me or mine. I've got mine, now go get yours. Society has tricked people into believing that successful people are self-made, especially this generation. You see, people post it all the time—self-made millionaires, but the truth is that someone helped them get there. You would think that would encourage them to give back, but instead, this generation is not trying to give anything to help anyone. We look at homeless people and turn the other way; we see single mothers with children, and instead of helping, we talk about them. We see young guys on the corner and just walk past them when we can make a difference. It is your obligation to God, yourself, and your generation to give back because if you don't, you are just adding to the problem. We can't walk away from the question: "Am I my brother's keeper?" We have to help because the answer is, "Yes, you are."

📍 GOD GIVES SEEDS TO THE SOWER

It's not by chance or accident that you actually made it. I say *actually* because we all know we have moments when we really didn't think this thing would happen. Just being honest, how many of us can say we still look around in disbelief like, "Wow, I can't believe I'm here"? I know I do. It was really by design when God had you in mind, and yes you are special. God chose you to be the one out of your family and your friends to be successful. Matthew 22:14, "For many are called, but few are chosen." He literally hand-picked you and said, "You are the one He will pour His blessing into so that you may pour it out into the world." Now the question is, where and what? You might be wondering who you should serve and what you should do. What can you give? There are a few things you can do. You can give your finances, give your time, share your influence, and pour out your spirit. Find the need and do your best to meet it. Also, when you think of giving back, don't think that you have to give out huge amounts of money. A lot of people use the excuse of not giving back because they don't have enough money. You can use what you have. God is not going to ask any more of you then what He knows you have because He's the one who gave it to you. Start where you are.

📍 BIG HEART BUT LITTLE POCKETS

I have always been a giver since I was a young boy. My heart always went out to those who were less fortunate. I grew up with the desire to help people, and I enjoy doing it whenever I'm given the opportunity. Shortly after I opened my business, there was a demand for me to help others, so I started to do little things to help and give back. The first thing was I started to go to different inner-city schools, including high schools and grammar schools, to speak to the students. It was my mission to motivate other inner-city youth that came from the same background as I did. My message was simple: "Your dreams are just one 'I can' thought away." I really encouraged the youth to remove "I can't" from their vocabulary and replace it with "I can." I did that for about two years, and it led me back to the military school that I graduated from. This was an amazing experience being back at Lincoln's Challenge. Seeing the chipped paint on the walls and the freshly buffed floors brought back so many memories. I could see me taking charge of my team as we fell into formation for morning roll call playing in my mind. "Team! Attention!" I said as I walked through the hall to meet with the director of the program. We walked over to the auditorium, and it was time for me to take the stage.

As I approached the stage, my heart was beating out of my chest. I gave my message. "Reality is wrong, and your dreams are right. A changed life starts with a changed mind." The purpose of this message was to encourage the students that despite your current situation, your dreams are real and they are possible, but in order to live them out, you must change your mindset and start believing. As I closed, I was met with a standing ovation, and it was at that moment I realized those students needed this. My contribution to them was to go back every class and give them a speech for free. As I continued to work with the program and speak to them, I noticed that some students were doing exceptionally well and wanted to go to college after graduation. So after praying about it, I started the MB Scholarship Fund where I donated one thousand dollars to their valedictorian that would go towards their first semester of school. This is what I meant by recommending that you start where you are and give what you have because the smallest assistance can make the world of difference. Every time I spoke it was for free, and it didn't cost me anything except a little bit of my time, but the words that were spoken could have very well changed someone's life. The intentions of my heart with the MB Scholarship Fund is for it to grow, and as my company grows, I want to be able to give one million dollars in scholarships to GED recipients to go to college. So get the thought, *I have to be rich to give back,* out of your mind and just start somewhere, and it will grow.

⚑ WHEN I WAS HUNGRY, YOU FED ME

Growing up in a single-family home with just my mother and four other siblings at the time was quite tough. There were a lot of times we had to go without. I can remember there were times when things had gotten really bad, and my mother wouldn't eat just to feed us. Yeah, times were tough, but I am grateful for those experiences because it taught me some valuable life lessons. It really taught me about helping others, about faith, and about sacrificing because even in our toughest times, my mother would still find a way to help others. She would open her home to people who had nowhere to go. Also, she would feed other children in the neighborhood who had nothing to eat. You wouldn't know it, but sometimes we were down to our last, and she would find a way to help someone else. It was hard at the time for me to comprehend when we were down to our last, why she wouldn't just worry about us. Every time I asked she would always quote this scripture taken from Luke 6:38, "Give and it shall be given unto you pressed down, shaken together, running over into your bosom shall men give unto you." I used to look at her like, what? I say that jokingly now, but honestly I couldn't understand that until I got older.

I realized that she was a blessing to others through her giving, and it set her up to be blessed as well. God honored her sacrifices, and whenever we got down to our last, someone from somewhere would be a blessing to her. In regard to faith, I remember one of the toughest times growing up. We had no lights and no gas in the house. My mother couldn't use the stove, and there was no hot water, so what she did was start a fire on two barbecue grills. On one she cooked bacon and eggs for breakfast, and on the other one, she set two pots of water. She took that water once it started boiling and put it in the bathtub and added a little soap and some cold water to get the right temperature, and she bathed us, fed us, and sent us off to school. What a strong woman. She didn't cry or fuss about the situation, not from what I can remember. She was setting an example of how to handle tough times in a godly way. As she was bent over the tub pouring that water on my head out of a kitchen bowl, she was singing, "Hold on, help is on the way. Hold on, help is on the way." This was one of her favorite songs, and on that morning during one of the hardest times of her life as a single mother of five, she stood there flat footed with her faith and encouraged herself in the Lord. "He may not come when you want Him, but He'll be right there on time. Oh, help is on the way." She sang as she got us dressed and sent us off to school. Oh, and guess what? There were extras from the breakfast she made and gave it to the friends I walked to school with. I said that to say this: As I grew, I held on to that moment because through it I learned that your giving should not be dictated by your current situation.

You must have it in your heart to give, even in your most trying times. Know that God sees you and He will honor your sacrifice. I remember one particular day while walking in downtown Chicago I was leaving a lunch meeting with one of my mentors, and I passed by a homeless man. He asked for some change for something to eat, and I told him that I didn't have any cash, but what I did have was some leftover food that I could give him. When I gave the food to him, it made his day, and the man was in tears. He said he hadn't eaten in three days, and people just walked past him as if he wasn't there, no one offering him any help. That experience stuck with me the whole day. Later that night in prayer, God had put it on my heart to feed the homeless. Let's talk about sacrifice. This was when times were a little rough in business—any business owner would understand this. One minute it's good, and the next it's bad. One minute there's some money, and the next you're robbing Peter to pay Paul. Basically, I didn't have many resources to pull from, but I knew what I heard from God, and I knew what my assignment was. So I talked with some of my friends, and we started to set things up to go out and feed the homeless.

At the time, I had no more than $250 to work with. So we went to the grocery store and purchased bread, meat, chips, and water. We got everything we needed to make lunch bags, so we went back to the shop, prayed over it, and started to assemble those bags. As we were making them, I had the homeless gentleman from downtown on my mind and started to sing. "Hold on help is on the way. Hold on, help is on the way." We worked all night getting the bags together, and somewhere in between packing them into boxes, we lost count. The next morning, we moved everything into three cars and headed down to the Pacific Garden Mission here in Chicago. When we arrived, we told the manager what we were planning to do, and they instructed the people inside to come outside where we were. We unloaded the cars and got into a circle around the food, locked hands, and prayed. "Father God, we heard your call, and here we are expecting a move from You. Get the glory on today as You use us to bless Your people. We ask that You increase and let us decrease in Jesus' name. Amen."

As we closed out our prayer, we started to pass out the bags, and to our amazement, we were able to feed five hundred people that day. It is so important that you do not let your life situation stifle you from responding to the voice of God in your giving. It is bigger than you. If I had allowed my financial situation to hold me back, five hundred people would have missed a meal that day. Be led by the Spirit of God and your heart to give and stand on your faith knowing that God will honor your sacrifice. God is so good, and we read in Hebrews 6:10, "God is not unjust; He will not forget your works and labor of love you have shown Him as you have helped His people and continue to help them."

⦿ GRAB MY HAND

When you have made it and have had the blessing of living in your destiny, oftentimes it comes with some form of platform. Whether it be public or private, God will put you in a position by meeting your destiny where He platforms you. There are those who gain notoriety and become known celebrities, and others gain positions of influence that may be on the job or through their business. Whatever it is, you must understand God didn't give you the platform to stand on by yourself. He wants to use that for His glory also. When you think of giving back, I don't want you to get stuck on giving financially; you can use your platform to pull others up. We're talking about creating opportunities. All through my life, I've been blessed to be able to meet the right people at the right time. It was God who strategically placed those people in my life. I was so blessed because, by some shape, form, or fashion, the Lord used their influence and platforms to help me get to the next level. They saw me reaching and weren't sitting so high up to where they couldn't reach down and help pull me up. Let that be a message to some to never get so high up to where you can't reach down to pull someone else up. Always remember you didn't just arrive. You had to get to where you are, and somebody helped you too.

As I grew my business, I held on to this notion of reaching to pull others up. I mean really, that's the whole point of the climb. One of the first people I was blessed to share my platform with was my brother. My mother taught us early to stick together, so quite naturally I didn't hesitate in regard to helping my brother. Growing up he made some mistakes that caused him to serve some time in prison, three and a half years to be exact. During the time he was incarcerated I had started to build the tattoo business and was doing very well. So one day during a phone conversation with him, he expressed his anxiety about coming home and starting his life. My brother was stressing about how he would find a job with a felony on his back. He was really concerned about how he was going to take care of himself. I remember telling him that day not to worry because I had something in mind. My brother and I have been artists since childhood, and I'll never tell him this, but he has always been the better one; keep that between us. Seriously, he has remarkable talent. He is truly the one who inspired my passion for art. I wanted to be as good as my big brother. So knowing this, I knew there was a seed in him, and I knew he could do this.

When God has given you a platform, you have to be able to see the seeds in people. They may not have it all together, they may have made some mistakes, but if God allows you to see their potential, it's your responsibility to help them. So finally, when he was released from prison, we immediately swung things into action. I started to teach him the craft of tattooing. I literally taught him everything I knew, and now he knew. I got him a seat working next to me in the shop and shared my clientele with him. If I had two clients that came in, he would take one, and I would take the other. I put him on my promotional publication, and I even had his face placed on the billboard I had put up on the highway. This is not to brag about what I did, but it's more so to show that when you are assigned to pull someone up, you have to gut yourself. Don't hold back. Pour out all the resources you can use so that the person you are helping will get the best opportunity that is possible. Long story short, my brother has gone on to build his own clientele and has become a household name here in Chicago. So the guy who had an X on his back and didn't have an opportunity in sight, but he was still reaching, is now making roughly about 80 to 100k a year doing what he loves. That's the blessing in giving back and by sharing your platform. You will be giving someone a chance at life, someone who wouldn't have had the opportunity had it not come through God and you. Don't let the devil trick you into being intimidated either by worrying about someone taking your spotlight.

There are a lot of stars in the sky, so there's enough room for everyone. God has all the stars in order, and He knows them all by name. So know that your position is good. God's got you right where He wants you, and no one can take your place. So take pleasure in pulling some other stars in the sky with you. After I saw the success of my brother and how the opportunity has blessed his life, I've since then started the Chicago Ink Tattooing 101 program. The CIT 101 program is a six-month apprenticeship program designed to teach young artist the fundamental foundation of body art. This program was created to give young artists the opportunities to work and express their art through another media. Also, it gives them a sense of entrepreneurship because each artist is conducting his or her own business.

We teach social media marketing, brand development, and leadership. This is in a part of the program called, "Attacking the Industry" in efforts to get the artist to think beyond the chair. We have put 15 artists through this program, and 11 are working today in their own respective places. Understand me when I say that it's bigger than you, I really mean bigger. You have traveled this road and have gone through hell and hot water, heartache, pain, and sleepless nights just to get here. I can imagine it was tough, believe me, I know, but I promise you it is all worth it. When you see the look on that person's face who's drowning in the pool of life, and you reach out your hand and say, "I got you," they'll remember you forever, and most importantly, God is pleased because you are in His will. As I close I want to say, "I love you, and I believe in you. You –can do this." You have come too far to turn back now, and you are too close to give up. Thank you for supporting and reading. Now put this book down and get to work.

- Malcolm Brown

About

Malcolm Brown:

What is Destiny? God's PURPOSE

Malcolm Brown is a Tattoo artist, entrepreneur, author, motivational speaker, and philanthropist. Malcolm, also widely known as "Dr. Solo Raw," is one of Chicago's most sought-after artists. He began his career on January 15, 2010, as an underground artist tattooing out of a bedroom in his mother's house. Despite starting at the bottom, he didn't stay there. He began climbing the ladder to the top. Because of his faith, tenacity, and drive, he soon became a household name throughout the city of Chicago and around the country. With clients spanning from coast to coast, Malcolm has planted his flag in the Tattoo industry as a leader, professional, and artist of influence. He currently sits on the board as founder and CEO of The TTL Group, a conglomerate of tattoo artists and business professionals whose mission is building a global brand and moving the industry forward.

Malcolm is the fourth of seven children, all raised by a single mother on the south side of Chicago. When asked about his childhood, Malcolm stated, "Growing up wasn't always easy—it got tough sometimes. There were a lot of things we had to go without, but I wouldn't trade that experience for the world. Those moments got me ready, and I wouldn't be the man I am today had I not gone through that. I'm thankful." Malcolm is very family oriented and sometimes stands as the glue that holds everyone together. He and his fiancé both live in Chicago and will be married in 2019.

He's a man with a message of resilience, encouraging others to go after their dreams and find their calling as motivational speakers. He also gives back in any way he can. Malcolm founded the MB Scholarship Fund dedicated to helping GED recipients with money to go to college. He's indeed a man who wears many hats, and as a new author, his mission is to share his story and messages with the world. When asked what's next, he replied, "I'm not sure. For years I've been building bridges from where I am to where I want to be, but I would always come home at night and find myself adding to my story. So I'll just say I'm a work in progress, but one thing's for sure—I'm pressing towards the mark." He's a young man with ambition as far as his eyes can see, dedicated to leaving a legacy and changing lives along the way.

EST. MMXV

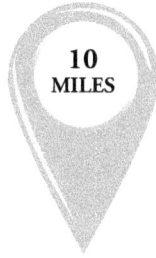

**10
MILES**

CONNECT WITH MALCOLM

Tmtydthebook@gmail.com

facebook.com/Solo Raw

Twitter: @soloraw

www.ingramcontent.com/pod-product-compliance
Lightning Source LLC
Chambersburg PA
CBHW071058090426
42737CB00013B/2379